To Lori,
With thanks for reading!
John Godfrey
22 March 2005.

THE
CANADA
WE WANT

{ COMPETING VISIONS FOR
THE NEW MILLENNIUM }

JOHN GODFREY
AND ROB McLEAN

Stoddart

Published in 1999 by Stoddart Publishing Co. Limited
34 Lesmill Road, Toronto, Canada M3B 2T6

Distributed by:
General Distribution Services Ltd.
325 Humber College Boulevard, Toronto, Ontario M9W 7C3
Tel. (416) 213-1919   Fax (416) 213-1917
Email customer.service@ccmailgw.genpub.com

03   02   01   00   99   1   2   3   4   5

Canadian Cataloguing in Publication Data

Godfrey, John F.
The Canada we want: competing visions for the new millennium

Includes bibliographical references and index.
ISBN 0-7737-3166-0

1. Canada — Forecasting.   2. Twenty-first century — Forecasts.
I. McLean, Rob, 1953–   .   II. Title.

FC635.G62 1999   971.064'8   C98-933089-3
F1034.2.G62 1999

Jacket Design: Bill Douglas @ The Bang
Text Design: Tannice Goddard

Printed and bound in Canada

*Stoddart Publishing gratefully acknowledges the Canada Council for the Arts and
the Ontario Arts Council for their support of its publishing program.*

To James, Kathleen, and Peter McLean,
Ian Godfrey,
and
Fraser Mustard,
a visionary Canadian

Disclaimer
Any criticisms of the present Government in Ottawa
were inserted at the insistence of Mr. McLean, who disowns
all of Mr. Godfrey's negative remarks about accountants,
and vice versa.

Contents

The Canada We Want

This is a book about rediscovering the Canada we want.

One hundred years ago, Canadians believed Wilfrid Laurier when he said the twentieth century belonged to them. Now, as we contemplate the beginning of a new century and a new millennium, no one would describe us as being in a particularly celebratory or cheerful mood. Canadians long to have a better country, but don't know how to get there, or whether we can get there from here. We know about the problems and the challenges. We have experienced frustration and anger. We would like to feel hopeful, but are perplexed by a set of curious paradoxes.

Paradox 1: Canada has, for five years now, been judged by the United Nations as the best place to live in the world. While vaguely conscious of this, Canadians have not got particularly excited about it, perhaps because we know better than anyone about the many underlying problems in our society that we have not yet solved. We're not confident this distinction is deserved or will last.

Paradox 2: Members of Canada's business elite have racked up more wealth in the 1990s than in any previous decade in Canada's history. Far from showing gratitude for this, a great many of them, aided by various regressive conservative politicians across the country, continue to mount a general attack on the social programs and public services that are the foundations of Canada's success as measured by the United Nations.

Paradox 3: The economic think-tank of the world's richest nations, the Organization for Economic Co-operation and Development, recently published a gloomy prediction about Canada's long-term economic prospects. The irony of this prediction is that for the last fifteen years, Canada has done just about everything a neo-conservative economist could want: implementing free trade, cutting budget deficits, lowering interest rates, privatizing public services, freezing the wages of public servants, reducing the size of government, cutting unemployment insurance and welfare benefits, and even starting to cut taxes.

Paradox 4: Some Canadians look at the recent years of deficit reduction and argue that we are tearing out the heart and soul of Canada. They feel betrayed by a federal Liberal government that has presided over the toughest and most sustained period of budget-cutting in Canadian history. Others look at the same picture and say that we haven't yet cut hard enough or deep enough — that we're still mollycoddling the unemployed and the welfare bums, and that we should keep slashing until we force them all back to work. Some believe that government is still too big and too fat, and that we need to privatize more and cut the rest down to size.

Paradox 5: We have the odd spectacle of the federal and provincial governments flirting with another round of constitutional negotiations without calling them constitutional negotiations. "We know Canadians don't want to hear anything more about the constitution," they must have said to each other, "but maybe they won't notice if we call these discussions 'renewing the social union' instead." Actually, this is not really a paradox. This is Canada.

If this were television, we could choose to wait and hope to hear a comforting announcer's voice saying, "Sorry, we are experiencing technical difficulties. Please do not adjust your set." Or we could change the channel. This book is our attempt to change the channel. It is not a lament for a nation, or a railing against recent policies and a call to reinstate the status quo ante. We would rather look ahead with hope than back in anger.

This book is about vision, ideas, and leadership. To realize the Canada we want demands of us a vision not simply of an improved Canada, but of a Canada that exists for a purpose. That purpose is to work together to produce the best society on earth.

Of course, no vision can ever become a reality without big ideas. Big ideas are what separate mere competence from greatness. In this book, we have tried to rediscover the big ideas of the past that inspired earlier generations of Canadians. We have also sought out the big ideas of our own generation of Canadians, and have attempted to present these ideas at some length in the words of their creators. And we have also recognized that there are some bad (at least to our taste) ideas floating around out there, ideas whose implementation would lead us to a Canada we don't want. Like dynamite, these bad ideas should be handled with care.

Vision and ideas, however, are not enough. Somebody has to take the ideas and translate them into action. This is the role of politicians at their most decisive. The phrase "conviction politician" describes a type of political leader driven by a clear agenda to change the existing order. Pierre Trudeau, Ronald Reagan, Margaret Thatcher, Preston Manning, Mike Harris, and Jacques Parizeau are all conviction politicians, whatever we may think of them personally, or of the quality of their ideas, or of the direction of their convictions. For the big ideas we present in this book to work, there will have to be both a hunger for them in the country and some political leaders with the understanding, enthusiasm, resolve, and sense of risk to implement them.

And finally there is timing. Is Canada ripe for big ideas? Or is this all there is . . . is this as good as it gets? We think that Canadians are poised for some new adventure, and that our souls are up for grabs.

Our souls will not be grabbed by more debate about the plumbing of Confederation — how much tax each level of government is entitled to levy, how much the federal government should transfer to the provinces, or whether educational new media fall under federal or provincial jurisdiction. This is all beside the point.

Let's argue instead about where we'd like to be by, say, 2017, and how we can get there. When we're celebrating Canada's 150th birthday, what do we want to be able to say about our accomplishments as a society? What kind of Canada do we want?

To have a fruitful debate about the Canada We Want and how to get there, we are compelled to attack the apostles of globalization, who attempt to persuade us to settle for something much less than even the Canada We Have, let alone the Canada We Want. A debate about where we want to be by 2017 would be sterile if, in fact, we don't have any choice in the matter — that is to say, if Canada is subject to external forces, such as globalization and technological change, that are so strong that resistance is futile.

Canadian businessman Conrad Black, British libertarian Ian Angell, and American-born novelist William Gibson offer us three versions of the Canada We Don't Want. Their views range from the relatively benign continentalist musings of Black to Gibson's absolutely hair-raising visions of the twenty-first century. But what all three share is a certain plausibility in their premises. If you run a worldwide business with a strong North American component, as Conrad Black does, what is more natural than to wish to rearrange the world's existing political and social arrangements to make business easier? If you observe, as Ian Angell does, that the world is increasingly seeking internationally footloose knowledge workers and shunning the rest of the labour force, why not push the argument to its logical conclusion by advocating the disappearance of the nation-state, which caters only to "losers"? If you believe that technology increasingly determines the fate of nations, why not go with William Gibson all the way to a world in which technology is all there is?

This is the Canada We Don't Want. But before we can have a useful discussion about the collective future we do want, we need to know where we're starting from. This is the purpose of our discussion of the Canada We Have, in which we argue that our society's finest accomplishments in the second half of the twentieth century have been a series of National Projects that have significantly improved the lives of all Canadians.

If there is one big idea that is central to this book, it is the concept of the National Project (which is why we have chosen to capitalize the term). We do not claim the idea as our own. Indeed, we argue that the concept, though it has had many other names, is as old as Canada itself. We think, however, that this term (which we did not consciously adopt from anyone else, but which has clearly occurred to others as well) is the most useful way to describe a series of collective national undertakings that have defined our history, created our present, and offer a model for our future.

What is a National Project? Public health insurance is an excellent example. Public health insurance evolved over a twenty-five-year period from an initiative that began in Saskatchewan in 1947 to a national program jointly funded by the federal and all provincial governments. It ensures that Canadians from every region of the country and every station in life have equitable access to the health care system. No one is denied medical treatment because he or she can't afford it. At the same time, as we shall see, the Canadian public health insurance system is inherently more efficient in economic terms than the American system of private insurance, and results in a significant competitive advantage for Canadian business.

What the health care example shows is that National Projects, as we understand them, are major undertakings that affect the lives of all

Canadians. They invariably involve both the federal and the provincial governments, and usually the private sector and community-based organizations as well. They typically evolve over a period of about two decades. They are of such a scope that they have both social and economic benefits for Canadian society. They have usually been above partisan politics, and have carried on through changes of government.

The post-war period — from about 1950 to the mid-1970s — was rich in National Projects. There were six: public health insurance and the expansion of the health care system; a massive investment in educational institutions; initiatives to enhance equality and income security, which created the social safety net; a major strengthening of human rights; a series of cultural policy initiatives that resulted in a great flowering of the creative arts; and a huge expansion of Canada's energy, transportation, and communications infrastructure.

We argue that the National Projects of the post-war era were all reflections of a particular understanding of the role that government should play in Canada. The legitimacy of that role has been called into question in the 1980s and 1990s. Given where we stand as a society, we believe this issue now needs to be revisited.

Crucial to our argument is a chapter discussing whether societies still can — and should — take collective action in the face of the pressures of globalization and the dominance of market-driven ideology around the world. We have entitled this chapter "Me versus Us," and in it we look at the new ideas that are challenging traditional assumptions about the left and the right, such as the Third Way and the fuller participation of civil society in national decision-making.

In the last quarter-century, National Projects have faded away, except in Quebec. There are a number of reasons for this, including government deficits and a general lack of confidence in the ability of governments to play the leadership role that is essential for successful National Projects. The question before us now is whether Canada should forever abandon this strategy for nation-building that was so successful in our collective past, or if, as we believe, it is time for a new wave of National Projects.

The bulk of this book is dedicated to exploring what new National Projects should be chosen; how we should go about implementing them; and how these National Projects could contribute to the well-being of Canadians, to the competitive advantage of Canada's economy within the limitations of sustainable development, and to national unity.

We believe that business people will appreciate that the National Projects we propose would all contribute to a significant strengthening of Canadian competitiveness and productivity. Implementing them does not require us to accept deficits, abandon debt reduction, or increase the size of government.

Those concerned about health care will recognize that we have an opportunity for a National Project that implements a proactive strategy to improve the developmental health of Canada's population as a whole, while reinvesting in the existing health care system.

Educators and multimedia professionals will understand that a properly designed National Project could make Canada the recognized world leader in educational new media, and in the process make lifelong learning a reality for all Canadians.

Environmentalists will be intrigued by a revolutionary new Canadian technology that generates electricity with no harmful emissions, creating the possibility of completely revisioning Canada's energy system. In a remarkably short period of time, we believe that such a National Project could move Canada from being a global leader in per capita energy use to being a global leader in providing solutions to some of the most serious problems threatening our planet's ecosystems.

And all Canadians should be interested in a National Project that could dramatically improve the prospects for Canada's children in a way that will yield major benefits for them as individuals, and hence for Canadian society as a whole.

None of these things can be accomplished by a business-as-usual attitude on the part of politicians, public servants, and indeed, citizens.

This is where bold and imaginative leadership is essential. In the past, many National Projects were led by the federal government. While we believe the federal government still has a key role to play, we think that in the future, leadership of National Projects should be more broadly shared. None of the National Projects we envision can be accomplished without the active participation of provincial governments, the private sector, and many of the organizations that make up Canada's civil society. In some cases, it is a provincial government that should take the lead, and the federal government that should play a supporting, facilitative role.

The National Projects we propose represent a fundamentally different approach to national unity. We don't need constitutional amendments to undertake them. Collectively, they add up to a compelling reason why, as we move into the first decades of a new century and a new millennium, we need and want more than ever a country called Canada.

2

The Canada We Don't Want

CONRAD BLACK'S VISION FOR CANADA

On various occasions, Conrad Black has suggested that Canada's future as a separate country is questionable, and that if Quebec ever separates, a union with the United States may be inevitable.

What Conrad Black thinks about Canada's future would not be important if he was still focused on hobnobbing with the upper classes in London, or on expanding his newspaper holdings in Israel and the U.S. Black now dominates the newspaper industry in Canada to an extent that was previously matched only by the Irving family's dominance of media in New Brunswick. By Black's own account, one of the most attractive aspects of the role of newspaper proprietor is the political influence and power that comes from controlling the editorial direction of newspapers that are read by millions of people. He is unabashed about having used that power in the past to support favoured people and causes. Anyone doubting this should read Black's autobiography, *A Life in Progress*. It can be found on the remainder tables in better Canadian bookstores for $3.99, which, if you can put up with turgid prose and perpetual damning with faint damns, is a great bargain.

From the lofty heights he has now attained, Black observes that "Canada is a matter of slight and rare curiosity to the great and turbulent world which it inhabits almost like an unwhimsical Pan among nations. On my returns I realize how far I have moved from the diffident, derivative, envious mood of the country, although I often think of Canada and the miraculous process of a full assumption of national consciousness. This, almost as much as economic reasons, is why I wanted to buy into Southam."

So there you have it, ladies and gentlemen. Through his newspapers, Conrad Black wants to help us achieve a full assumption of national consciousness.

The curious thing is that the national consciousness he apparently wishes Canada to assume is one that is stripped of the things that many believe are important distinctions between the societies of Canada and the United States. For example, Black complains at length about social policies that are designed to reduce inequality in Canadian society. He observes that "U.N. surveys were doubtless correct in putting Canada and Denmark at the top of advantageous places to live, but not for the most ambitious, exceptional people who give a nation its character."

What is Conrad Black's vision for Canada? There appear to be two versions. One is the continentalist vision — gradually forming closer political ties with the U.S. — which has been discussed in various speeches and articles over the past decade. For example, in a 1992 article in the *National Interest*, Black argues that "Canada's natural and human wealth, together with its geographical position, make it an area so strategic that the world will be more than passingly curious to see if concern for universal public-sector medicare, strict gun-control, and a few other public policy and folkloric distinctions (which could be accommodated in a fuller embrace with the United States anyway) will suffice to prevent a continentalist political process from succeeding as a sequel to the economic foundation of free trade."

The odd thing about his continentalist vision is that Black has apparently neglected to consider the politics of a Canada-U.S. union from the American point of view. In the spectrum of U.S. political opinion, even most Reform voters would be classified as "liberals." What is the probability of the U.S. agreeing to accept thirty million new citizens, the majority of whom would vote with the Democrats and, unlike most Americans, could be counted on to show up at the polls? As part of the United States, Canada would have more electoral college votes in presidential elections than any other state in the Union except California. There is no possibility that American politicians would accept an alliance with Canada unless it could be demonstrated that Canadians had adopted the same perspectives and voting habits as Americans.

The second, less extreme version of Conrad Black's vision for Canada — Americanizing Canada — is described in "Taking Canada Seriously," an article that appeared in the Winter 1997-98 edition of the *International Journal*. In this article, Black takes pains to downplay the differences between Canada and the U.S. "A nationality cannot define itself by its social programmes, " he argues. He observes that "the distinction between English-speaking Canadians and their nearest American neighbours is a good deal subtler than that which exists in the United States between Texas and New England or the Great Plains and California."

Here is Black's prescription for Canada's future.

[Canada] has an opportunity to blend the British monarchical tradition of benign paternal government and the French civil law system of rights and obligations with the culture of American enterprise and individualism, with which all Canadians are familiar- through osmosis if nothing else. We must devise a tax structure that creates incentives and rewards enterprise. We must restore private medicine, fund and encourage academic excellence, especially of the politically incorrect variety . . .

As part of our reformed Canadian constitutional arrangements, the position of governor general, which is now an imperial anomaly, should be reclassified as president and governor general. It should be given more authority, somewhat on the model of the French presidency which, as devised by Charles de Gaulle, combines republican and monarchical aspects, and should be filled by direct popular election.

While retaining a comparatively generous safety net for less advantaged people, we must shift our emphasis to attract and retain in Canada successful and highly motivated people in all useful fields. If we wish any worthwhile identity, we have to mobilise our resources and reorder our society to encourage the exceptional rather than reinsure the under-achievers. Of course we must not forget the less fortunate, but we have been running the risk, to borrow an undiplomatic phrase from the German chancellor, of having the whole national convoy proceed at the pace of the slowest ship.

In short, this second version of Conrad Black's vision is that Canada should become more like the U.S., if not join the U.S. Even Black admits that most Canadians don't share this vision today. Perhaps he hopes that with his new *National Post* newspaper, he can change our minds.

However, we should not be too quick to accept Black's fundamental premise: that a "nationality cannot define itself by its social programmes." This assertion begs the question: What does define a nationality? In today's cosmopolitan societies, it cannot be the things that used to differentiate nationalities — such as language or place of birth. In today's world, nationalities are defined by politics and culture. The political systems of Canada and the U.S. have many similarities, but also differences that stem from a different understanding of the role of government in relation to the individual and society.

Black has it exactly wrong: a nationality is precisely defined by its social programs. That is, a nationality is defined by its perception of the mutual obligations that exist among members of a society, how those obligations are articulated through the political process, and how they are communicated through arts, literature, and popular culture.

Canada and the U.S. share many aspects of popular culture, but the differences, though subtle, are crucial, despite the fact that Black ridicules them as "folkloric." For example, Canadian politeness may be a cliché, but it is also symbolic of our recognition of the mutual obligations that exist between the individual and the broader society. As another example, consider the difference between a David Letterman monologue and the brilliant satire of "This Hour Has 22 Minutes." True political satire, as opposed to crude one-liners, barely exists in the U.S., but it is alive and well in Canada. Satire is effective only within a society in which those who aspire to lead retain a clear understanding of their obligations to their fellow citizens. That cabinet ministers, the leaders of the opposition parties, and even Prime Minister Chrétien have collaborated in the satire is a sign of a political culture that is far healthier than one in which politicians are treated as celebrities.

Conrad Black says that it is "the most ambitious, exceptional people who give a nation its character." Again, he has it exactly wrong. Canada's character is not defined by celebrities, let alone by the type of business person best characterized by Fraser Mustard as a "fiscal roulette player." (Some business people create wealth for their society; fiscal roulette players merely rearrange it.) Rather, Canada's character is made manifest in the great National Projects of the post-war era. In combination, these projects define a society that is in important respects radically different from that of our great neighbour to the south.

Conrad Black seems to think that Canada is a failure, that this failure can be traced to the social policies of the post-war era, and that the solution is to encourage Canada to become more like the United States. Again, he has it exactly wrong. Canada owes its success as a society largely to the National Projects of the post-war era. The evidence shows that Canadians would not benefit from becoming more like Americans. Rather, it is Americans who would benefit if the U.S. became more like Canada.

Some argue, however, that this is all beside the point, and that we are now all subject to global forces that no country can resist. Enter Mr. Ian Angell.

ANGELL'S PROPHECY

Back in 1993, the *Guardian* newspaper in Britain published this riddle: "What's the difference between Zambia and Goldman Sachs? One is an African country that makes $2.2 billion a year and shares it among 25 million people. The other is an investment bank that makes $2.6 billion . . . and shares it among 161 people. FAIR ENOUGH!" If this is your kind of world, then Ian Angell is your kind of guy.

Ian Angell? Who's he, and why should we care? Angell is a professor of information systems at the London School of Economics who has taken to writing dyspeptic articles about the future of the world. His titles give the game away: "The Information Revolution and the Death of the Nation-state: For Life, Liberty and Property"; "The Signs Are Clear: The Future Is Inequality"; "Winners and Losers in the Information Age."

It is tempting to dismiss Angell as one of those deliberately provocative, professionally grumpy dons who play so well on British TV. But he is worth paying attention to for three reasons. First, his ideas are attracting attention, particularly with the publication of his new book, *The Barbarian Manifesto*. Second, there is enough truth in the starting point of his argument to make the whole thing worth considering. And finally, the spirit of his analysis is so joyfully mean-spirited that counterattack is irresistible.

The point of departure for his thesis is a set of ideas that has been advanced by eminently reasonable people like Peter Drucker and Robert Reich. In "The Age of Social Transformation," a widely noted piece written for the *Atlantic Monthly* in 1994, Drucker argued that just as industrial workers had replaced farmers and domestic servants in the early twentieth century, by the year 2000 traditional blue-collar workers will have become "auxiliary employees," replaced by technologists and knowledge workers. But there is a problem. "The great majority of the new jobs require qualifications the individual worker does not possess and is poorly equipped to acquire," he wrote. "Displaced industrial workers thus cannot simply move into knowledge work or services the way displaced farmers and domestic workers moved into industrial work." Nor will developing countries be able to continue to base their progress on the comparative advantage of having cheap industrial labour.

For his part, Robert Reich predicts that in the Information Age there will be three categories of work: symbolic-analytical services (the knowledge workers who are the problem-identifiers, -solvers, and -brokers), in-person services, and routine production services. These last two categories are what Angell lumps together as service workers.

Knowledge workers versus service workers equals, in Angell's world, winners versus losers. "FAIR ENOUGH!" says Angell, because service workers are a net loss to the state and to corporations, which is why companies are downsizing and fighting to reduce wages. Knowledge workers, by contrast, are the real generators of wealth and are welcome anywhere in the world. In Britain and the United States, he notes, foreign entrepreneurial investors are fast-tracked as immigrants. Angell also cites the example of Canada's thousand-dollar head tax on those seeking landed immigrant status, which he says sends "a message which is likely to reduce applications from poor service workers but increase applications from rich knowledge workers."

So far there is a familiar and uncomfortable air of truth in what Angell says. When he claims that knowledge workers feel more and more undervalued and betrayed by the nation-state, and that their skills are in increasing demand by global companies, who among us cannot think of talented Canadians lured south by American multinationals? In the States, and especially in places like Silicon Valley in California, highly paid technology workers have access to better health care, schools, and other aspects of the social infrastructure, basically because they can afford to pay for it privately. And for every one of us who might feebly respond that Canada's stable and high-quality lifestyle compensates for the higher salaries and more generous benefits available in the United States, there is a Rob Burgess, chief executive officer of Macromedia Inc. of San Francisco. In an interview in the *Globe and Mail* in June 1998, the Canadian-born Burgess said clean streets and green parks were not much of a lure for high-tech workers. In fact, Burgess claimed it was easy for him to recruit his fellow Canadians. Of his homeland, he said, "I feel it's a Third World country. . . . The United States is a high-tech country."

Angell argues that increasing numbers of footloose knowledge workers are already forcing nation-states to lower top tax rates to attract and keep their elite. He foresees that companies will negotiate preferential tax deals not only for themselves but also for chosen upper-echelon employees. Meanwhile, the amount of disposable income for the rest of society will decline drastically. The tax burden will shift "irrevocably onto the shoulders of the immobile; and away from income and onto expenditure." When Leona Helmsley said "only the little people pay taxes," she was simply making a prediction, says Angell approvingly.

Lest this seem some wildly futuristic scenario, consider the November 1997 report from the respectable Organization for Economic Co-operation and Development (OECD), which called on the Canadian government to cut income taxes to prevent highly skilled Canadians from being lured to lower-tax jurisdictions such as the United States. Yet the OECD, which is the international club for the world's richest nations, admitted that in the larger scheme of things, Canada's overall tax burden is not unreasonable. Tax revenue represents about 36 percent of Canada's gross domestic product (GDP), which is lower than in Europe. Canada also has the lowest payroll taxes of any OECD country, including the U.S., even when the premiums for Employment Insurance, the Canada Pension Plan, and Workers' Compensation are included.

Taking a leaf out of Angell's book, the OECD proposed changes to the Canadian tax mix so that Ottawa would get more revenue from consumption and payroll taxes and less from corporate and personal taxes. These changes are necessary, said the OECD, because of globalization. Canada needs "to streamline the tax system so the private sector is better prepared to respond" to the challenges of trade liberalization and competition from low-wage countries. In fact, it is the United States, not the rest of the world, that is forcing the pace of tax change in Canada, because it is the United States that is attracting highly skilled, high-income earners, including entrepreneurs and innovators. The United States has lower federal income taxes and is proposing a reduction in capital gains taxes.

Meanwhile, in both the United States and Canada, profits are already rising and wages falling, even without the OECD's proposed changes. The Washington, D.C.-based Economic Policy Institute recently issued a report showing that in the 1990s, income has been redistributed from labour to owners of capital as profitability has reached historically high levels. Increasing wage inequality in the 1980s and 1990s has forced middle- and low-wage earners to accept reductions in their real wages.

In Canada, the "recovery," which began in 1992, saw corporate profits swallow 44.8 percent of the increase in national income between 1992 and the first quarter of 1995. Since corporate profits have averaged about 10 percent of total national income over the past twenty years, the increase in profits has been much larger than the total increase in wages and salaries. And the money was not ploughed back into increasing productive capacity. Instead, annual dividends paid out to foreign shareholders jumped from $1 billion in 1992 to $12 billion in 1995.

As for the future of the nation-state, Angell says it will mutate into another kind of organization, "which will delegate market regulation to continent-wide bodies such as the North American Free Trade Agreement or the European Union, which in turn will use their economic muscle and conspire with local communities to undermine each member state." The new successful nations will be non-democratic city-states like Hong Kong or Singapore. Liechtenstein and Monaco are on their way in Europe. Why not Lisbon or London? Indeed, why not simply avoid geographically defined states altogether and head for cyberspace ("the greatest tax haven of them all, Bermuda in the sky with diamonds," in the arresting phrase of British journalist William Rees-Mogg)? Already there are trillions of dollars in hot money from the black-market economy, from narco-dollars to tax-flight money, "sloshing around the world financial markets, in effect gambling against national economies and profiting from the numerous mistakes of their politicians."

Echoing Nietzsche, Angell says, "Many too many are born. The state was devised for the superfluous ones." Successful states of the future, he argues, will ensure that there is a high proportion of wealth-generating knowledge workers to wealth-depleting service workers, a strategy Angell calls "rightsizing."

And as for politics, "Democracy," asserts Angell, "is bad for business." In the Information Age, "governments chosen by the majority are governments chosen by losers." In fact, in his latest writings and interviews, Angell sounds increasingly like some strange throwback to not only Nietzsche but also Ayn Rand. "Western politicians are pandering to the masses. But the masses will not win in the natural selection for dominance of an increasingly elitist world. Information technology . . . has increasingly liberated the talented few from the restrictions of the three dimensions of physical space and from the tyranny of the masses. It has freed the elite from the constraint, the mind-set and the moralities of the collective."

But the most powerless creatures of all are democratic politicians, he says. "How have the pathetic politicians lost control over the course of events? How is it that they stand before us with sham, bluster, superficiality and panic, while their old certainties are falling apart?" According to Angell, "Their jobs along with those of so many of their voters will go the same way as the Age they represent."

Such is the cheerless world-view of Ian Angell. How are we to react to such ideas? Given the body of evidence that underlies at least the premise of his argument, we would be wrong simply to dismiss him out of hand. Rather, we should view his world as a dystopia, a place where we don't want to live. And we should use his ideas as a springboard for thinking about the place where we do want to live. To do this, we must start by asking ourselves what's wrong with this picture. Obviously, from the viewpoint of traditional Western liberal and humanitarian values, there is plenty wrong. But what about the facts and trends to which he refers? Is this a true portrayal of the way the world is going? And if we don't like or accept this unbrave new world, what can we do to change our destiny in such a place?

There is clearly plenty of evidence to support Angell's world-view, whether it is the OECD arguing for lower taxes in Canada to discourage the brain drain or the arguments raised by four of Canada's largest chartered banks in support of mergers. At a more profound level, Angell's picture is also true if we choose to believe certain things about our fellow human beings and about human society. The picture is true if we believe that individualism is the highest good. It is true if we believe that the chief goal of life is economic maximization — a goal more important than family, community, society, culture, or justice; more important than kindness, faith, and love.

If we believe that community doesn't matter, that people move to wherever they can earn the highest salary, then the picture is true. If we think, like that dusty libertarian Ayn Rand, that selfishness is the highest purpose of human life, then this vision is for us. This picture is also true if we take an accountant's view of humankind: that we are all either an economic liability or an economic asset, and that there is very little we can do, either as a society or as individuals, to alter our status, to cross the balance sheet, to change our fate.

But if we don't see ourselves in this picture, or don't want to, if we actually have faith in human beings, if we believe that where we live and work matters, and that we do not live for money alone, then it is time to think very carefully about the kind of world, and the kind of Canada, we want in the future.

So what is the alternative vision, the answer to Ian Angell? What kind of a world and a country do we really want? Perhaps the great ice storm that ravaged southern Quebec and eastern Ontario in January 1998 reminds us graphically of the country we both need and long for. Writing at the time in the *Globe and Mail*, Jeffrey Simpson put it well:

> Somehow in these trying times the pettiness of politics fades before the larger requirements of solidarity. Even the secessionists in Quebec have praised federal efforts, including that of the army, in that stricken province.
>
> Without anyone drawing attention to the fact, the federal response reminded Quebecers — as it reminded Manitobans when the Red River was submerged — of the benefits of being part of a larger community in which risk and effort are shared. Federalism, at its bare minimum, is like an insurance policy, representing the pooling of risk and benefit.
>
> Community, then, flows from concentric circles, moving out from family to neighbours, from municipalities to regions, from provinces to nation, and to the extent that help arrived from the United States, from nation to continent. It is heartwarming in difficult times to know that people do sense a feeling of interdependence and that the benefit of being part of these concentric circles of community is the sharing of burdens.
>
> Put another way, in our highly rights-driven society with its pervasive discourse of "rights talk," hardly anybody mentions the notion of responsibility, or what we owe each other. A crisis such as this ice storm arrives — or the Manitoba and Saguenay floods — and suddenly rights yield to responsibilities because community trumps individualism.

One name we give to this alternative vision of community is civic society. Civic society connotes solidarity, not exclusion; unity, not division. Civic society rejects the concept of winners and losers in favour of mutual responsibility and social cohesion. Civic society demands more civic engagement, not less. Community is the essence of civic society. Civic society stresses the equality and moral autonomy of all its citizens. Civic society builds democracy through more involved citizens. In short, civic society is the antithesis of everything Ian Angell represents, and civic society must be the foundation of the Canada We Want.

Having said that, what if Angell is right, and the forces of globalization are too powerful for Canada to resist? To get a picture of where this leads, we turn to William Gibson.

GIBSON'S SPRAWL

Compared with William Gibson, Conrad Black and Ian Angell are pikers. In his first three novels, known as the Sprawl trilogy, Gibson paints a picture of a future world that is more radical, ruthless, and realistic than the futures advocated by Black or Angell.

William Gibson is a science-fiction writer who was born and raised in the southern United States but moved to Canada in 1967 during the Vietnam War. He ended up in Vancouver in 1972, and has lived there ever since. He rose to prominence in 1984 when his first novel, *Neuromancer*, won all three of the major science-fiction awards: the Hugo Award, the Philip K. Dick Memorial Award, and the Nebula Award.

In *Neuromancer*, and subsequently in *Count Zero* (1986) and *Mona Lisa Overdrive* (1988), Gibson paints an astonishingly vivid picture of the world in the not-too-distant future. Gibson's accomplishment is to extrapolate and weave together many of the trends we see in society today. His writing is so powerful precisely because we can see around us the accumulating evidence that the world he has created is a dark but plausible description of how our children and grandchildren might live.

Neuromancer begins in the dangerous streets of the Chiba district of Tokyo, and then moves to the Sprawl, the continuous urban corridor down the U.S. Eastern Seaboard otherwise known as BAMA, the Boston-Atlanta Metropolitan Axis. After a brief adventure in Istanbul, the scene shifts to Freeside, the ultimate tourist destination, located only a short shuttle-ride away in space.

Ian Angell might call the principal protagonist in *Neuromancer* a knowledge worker, but he's really a data thief:

Case was twenty-four. At twenty-two, he'd been a cowboy, a rustler, one of the best in the Sprawl. He'd been trained by the best, by McCoy Pauley and Bobby Quine, legends in the biz. He'd operated on an almost permanent adrenaline high, a byproduct of youth and profi-ciency, jacked into a custom cyberspace deck that projected his dis-embodied consciousness into the consensual hallucination that was the matrix. A thief, he'd worked for other, wealthier thieves, employ-ers who provided the exotic software required to penetrate the bright walls of corporate systems, opening windows into rich fields of data.

The matrix, otherwise known as cyberspace (a term Gibson coined), is the Internet on steroids — a vast inner space created through a continu-ous stream of legitimate and illegal transactions and data exchanges among interconnected computers throughout the planet, and beyond. Dominat-ing the matrix are the databanks of major corporations, pro-tected by ICE — intrusion countermeasures electronics. Corporations dominate the societal landscape as well, competing in ruthless techno-wars. Top entertainers and scientists are, in effect, owned by their corporate employers. One of the main subplots in *Count Zero* is the attempt of a leading scientist to escape, at the risk of his life, from his position with one corporation and transfer his allegiance to another.

Government in Gibson's world is conspicuous by its absence — the state seems to have withered away completely. About the only reference to government in *Neuromancer* occurs when Case's bodyguard, Molly, describes what she had to do to afford the surgery that gave her augmented eyesight and scalpel blades implanted under each fingernail like a cat's claws. She had a "cut-out chip" implanted in her nervous system so she could work as a prostitute without having to be conscious while turning tricks. Then the cut-out chip started to malfunction, and she woke up as a participant in a snuff scene.

> "I came up. I was into this routine with a customer. . . ." She dug her fingers deep in the foam. "Senator, he was. Knew his fat face right away. We were both covered with blood. We weren't alone. She was all . . ." She tugged at the temperfoam. "Dead. And that fat prick, he was saying, 'What's wrong. What's wrong?' 'Cause we weren't finished yet . . ."
> She began to shake.
> "So I guess I gave the Senator what he really wanted, you know?" The shaking stopped. She released the foam and ran her fingers back through her dark hair. "The house put a contract out on me. I had to hide for a while."

Government also makes a single appearance in *Johnny Mnemonic*, a Gibson short story that was made into a movie in 1995. One of the characters is Jones, a dolphin that was augmented with electronics so it could detect enemy submarines during the last war with Russia. Johnny is told that if he bribes Jones with heroin, the dolphin will be willing to use his electronically enhanced sonar to read the data locked into his head and find the password necessary to release it. "How does a cybernetic dolphin get wired to smack?" Johnny Mnemonic asks. "The war," Molly replies. "They all were. Navy did it. How else you get 'em working for you?"

The majority of the population is kept amused and distracted by drugs and "simstim," short for simulated stimuli. Top simstim stars employed by the broadcaster Sense/Net are equipped with artificial eyes and special sensors that record what they see and feel. These recordings can be replayed on simstim decks that give the user the illusion of being in the star's body. In *Mona Lisa Overdrive*, Mona is unknowingly a pawn in a plot to kidnap one of the top simstim stars, Angie.

> The Angie stims were still sealed in plastic. Mona took one at random, slit the wrapper with her thumbnail, slotted it, and put the trodes on. She wasn't thinking; her hands seemed to know what to do, friendly animals that wouldn't hurt her. One of them touched PLAY and she slid into the Angie-world, pure as any drug, slow saxophone and limo glide through some European city, how the streets revolved around her, around the driverless car, broad avenues, dawn-clean and almost empty, with the touch of fur against her shoulders, and rolling on, down a straight road through flat fields, edged with perfect, identical trees.

From a distance, the world of Gibson's Sprawl series is fascinating, but none of the people who live in that world are having much fun. Any enjoyment the main characters have is ephemeral, and is triggered by drugs, sex, jacking into cyberspace, or revenge. Society as such doesn't exist; rather, there are multiple subcultures coexisting within an anarchistic space. Quality of life is determined largely by wealth and, for some, the ability to manipulate technology. Gibson's unique prose reflects the world he has created: frenetic, tense, terse, stoned, jacked-in, paranoid, sardonic.

Gibson's vision is the logical extension of the world that Ian Angell advocates and, if you extrapolate far enough, of the Canada that Conrad Black apparently wants. To be fair, Black would dispute that his vision for Canada has anything to do with Gibson's Sprawl. However, the world Gibson describes reflects what already exists in the underclass and punk cultures of major U.S. cities. Oddly enough, even though the Sprawl series novels were all written in Vancouver, there are no references to Canada in any of the three books. None at all. Is this accidental? Or is William Gibson trying to tell us something?

We could go on, but these three examples suffice to describe the Canada We Don't Want. We admire Gibson's work immensely, but we don't want to live there. We fear that Angell is right about the forces that are under-mining the state, but we disagree that the proper response is to capitulate. While we share much of Black's admiration for the United States, and appreciate the States as a great and mostly good neighbour, we don't think the solution to any of Canada's problems is American-style individualism. Furthermore, we have the evidence to prove it, in the next chapter.

3

The Canada We Have

In September 1998, the United Nations proclaimed Canada the best country in the world to live in for the fifth year in a row. Canada was measured on the Human Development Index, which rates the achievements of a country in three basic dimensions of human development.

The first dimension is longevity — how long people live — which is a proxy for the overall health of the population. The measure used is life expectancy at birth — that is, how long a baby born today is expected to live, based on current trends. In this category, Canada scores third highest in the world behind Japan and Iceland. The second dimension is knowledge. It is measured by a combination of adult literacy and education. Here, Canada scores highest in the world. The third dimension is standard of living, measured by the size of the economy divided by the population. Here, Canada scores fourth, behind the U.S., Japan, and Norway. The combination of all three dimensions puts Canada in the lead.

This chapter argues that the foundations for Canada's success in the

1990s, as measured by the U.N., were laid in the extraordinary period roughly between 1950 and 1975. Looking back, we can count six great National Projects: public health insurance and the health care system; education; income security; human rights; Canadian culture and research; and physical infrastructure.

In order to understand these National Projects, we first need to explore the abiding national attitudes and values that prompted Canadians to support them. Clearly, there was something in the national psyche predating the Second World War that not only permitted but also encouraged this kind of national institution-building.

In his recent book on Canada at the end of the twentieth century, *Reflections of a Siamese Twin*, John Ralston Saul offers a provocative and stimulating reinterpretation of Canadian history, and in doing so, puts these national attitudes and values into a useful, if unorthodox, historical context.

Saul's particular purpose is to challenge the orthodoxy of globalization, which we discussed in the previous chapter. His views on Canada's economic history are a delightfully perverse and intellectually compelling response to the apostles of the inevitability of the forces of globalization. In essence, Saul argues that Canada is a fundamentally poor country. While there is some good farmland and a lot of natural resources, that kind of economic base does not produce a stable, balanced economy for most countries. On the contrary, commodity-based economies are usually subject to incessant, devastating swings. Furthermore, the value of our farmland is severely reduced by Canada's climate, and the country has always lacked a critical density of population. "This sort of economy almost invariably produces an extreme social divide between a few rich and many poor," writes Saul.

But Canada somehow avoided this fate. Why? Because economic prosperity grew out of social equilibrium, and not the other way round. This is a hugely important point, one central not only to Saul's argument but also to ours. Saul argues that the simple feat of survival in a difficult northern place meant favouring cooperation over competition. Thus there was a fundamental economic imperative for creating an egalitarian society "marked by an individualism which was understood to mean cooperate or perish." But this egalitarianism grew beyond a mere survival mechanism, and led to early and active government involvement in the economy, from land settlements and railway building to the establishment of social programs such as universal public education, which began in 1852 in Prince Edward Island.

Mid-nineteenth-century politicians like Louis-Hippolyte LaFontaine also clearly understood the connection between this social value and the fundamental nature of the Canadian political system. "The only way in which [the authorities] can prevent us from succeeding is by destroying the social equality which is the distinctive characteristic of much of the population of Upper Canada as of Lower Canada," he once said. "This social equality must necessarily bring our political liberty. . . . No privileged caste can exist in Canada beyond and above the mass of its inhabitants."

Another element in this distinctively Canadian brand of egalitarianism has been our long-standing dedication to the principle of wealth re-distribution, first among individuals, then among regions, through transfer payments. "These three elements — public education, government intervention in both social and economic structures, and transfer payments — allowed us to build prosperity on the foundations of systemic poverty," writes Saul. "And it was on the basis of the social equilibrium created by these policies that the business sector was able to blossom."

The history of Canada, says Saul, is characterized by a balance between individual rights and collective rights. "In other words, we were faced by a choice over the meaning of individualism. Did it mean opportunity, or a combination of opportunity and results? The Canadian government favoured the latter. That this combination put limits on the possibilities attached to both opportunity and results was merely an expression of the more cooperative tradition of egalitarianism in Canada." He goes on to say, "In Canada, the restrictions of northern poverty, low population density and difficult geography have meant that great individual initiative will always be needed, but so will great public initiative."

Because Canada has always had to balance the competing forces of individual and public initiative, as well as constantly juggle the interests of its three founding peoples, one of the defining characteristics of the nation has been its complexity. Complexity demands more of citizens than simplicity. Complexity demands thought. "The assumption of complexity is a search for balance between different elements; not eradication or domination of one over the others, but a continuing struggle to maintain some kind of equilibrium," asserts Saul.

The greatest internal threat to Canada has always come from those who have held out the false promise of simple solutions, whether those simple solutions have come from Quebec separatists or Western populists. The latest threat comes from those who argue for the simplicity of a market-driven economic imperative imposed upon us by the imperative of globalization. "Suddenly people with responsibilities are saying *globalization*, the way they used to say *homeland* and once said *heaven*. The marketplace is evoked with the tones of racial purity. They sing the praises of competition — of their forceful ability to compete — the way they once sang those of their national language. And the salesmen of trade have taken up the old nationalist military vocabulary. . . . At least this is a less bloody form of self-indulgence. But it is still built on mythological simplicity, not on the complexities of reality, that is to say, of society."

The greatest contributions to building Canada, says Saul, have always come from those who have preached and practised the difficult art of reconciliation. Saul invokes the spirit of reconciliation that animated the Quebec Act of 1774, the Constitution Act of 1791, the cooperation of the Lower Canada and Upper Canada rebels in 1837 and that of the reform leaders of 1840-51. We abandon the work of two centuries of reconciliation at our peril. "If we do this . . . what forces will be unleashed? Or rather, will incalculable, uncontrollable forces be released?"

So what must Canadian governments do to preserve the spirit of reconciliation and balance, to maintain our social and political equilibrium?
Saul quotes a paragraph from the report of the Rowell-Sirois Commission
on Dominion-Provincial Relations, which began its work in the late
1930s. "Collective action through the agency of democratic government
implies a common purpose and an agreed method of achieving it," wrote
the report's authors. "If the common endeavour is one with respect to
which deep impulses in the community arouse differing conceptions, it is
likely to break down and the subsequent disharmony will embarrass all
the common enterprises which have been entrusted to the government."

A "common purpose and an agreed method of achieving it" can
be attained only by government first thinking through the purpose and
the method, then working with citizens to enlist their support. In such
an approach, the roles of ideas and public policy become crucial. In a
felicitous phrase, Saul describes Canada as "a coalition of ideas based on
an assumption of the public good."

So what is holding us back? "Our problem," answers Saul, "is not a
lack of policy, but rather an inability to believe that such a thing as long-
term, integrated policy could still have a place in Canada; particularly
policy which responds to the particularities of the place." We are so
mesmerized by ideas developed elsewhere that we mistake them for eternal
truths. Saul quotes with approval Canadian economist Harold Innis, who
kept arguing in favour of "an economics which derived its laws from
the history of the place, rather than deriving the place from a set of
all-purpose laws formulated in Britain." Saul himself argues that the most
crucial need for long-term, integrated policy is in the area of social policy,
and that if we were to address the social situation collectively and nationally, we would not only develop a sense of positive nationalism, but also
put paid to the idea that only Quebec is capable of developing a progressive social agenda.

Finally, Saul argues that "Canada was built over a century and a half
through eight dramatic strategic acts." These great acts range in nature

from the political (the Baldwin-LaFontaine handshake in 1842), to the economic (the building of the transcontinental railway, the National Policy), to the social (mass immigration, social programs), to the cultural (the Official Languages policy), but they share the common feature of being deliberate, strategic acts of nation-building. It is the premise of this chapter, and indeed this book, that only through the planning and implementation of such great strategic acts or National Projects in the future can Canada survive the rigours of globalization, and give the lie to the apostles of the Canada We Don't Want.

Before we look ahead, however, let us remind ourselves of how we became the best society in the world.

HEALTH CARE FOR ALL

Public health insurance, and what it stands for, is today one of the cornerstones of Canadian society. Before 1947, it didn't exist. Back then, the stress of a serious illness in the family was compounded by the potential for a financial catastrophe. Private health insurance was available only for those who could afford it.

It is hard for Canadians to appreciate the level of stress and worry that exists for the majority of people in the world, who either cannot afford proper care or are forced to make enormous financial sacrifices because of an illness or accident. Even in the U.S., getting and maintaining private health insurance is a major issue for most people. Many are not able to change jobs or move to a new city because they risk losing their health insurance coverage if they do. Many more can't get the services they need because their health insurance company won't pay for them.

So how did Canadians get public health insurance? In 1945, anticipating the end of the Second World War, the federal government presented an ambitious proposal to the provinces at a dominion-provincial conference. Among other things, the proposal was designed to pre-empt a post-war recession and introduce a new social order. In essence, the federal government proposed that the provinces surrender certain taxation powers (which had been suspended temporarily by the war) in return for subsidies, greater federal contributions to old-age pensions and unemployment insurance, and the assumption by Ottawa of 60 percent of the cost of a new health insurance scheme that would be operated by the provinces.

This proposal went nowhere at the time. However, in 1947, the Co-operative Commonwealth Federation government of Saskatchewan introduced Canada's first public insurance plan for hospital services. In 1956, the federal government offered to cost-share public hospital insurance with the provinces on a fifty-fifty basis. By 1961, all provinces and territories had taken up this offer.

Saskatchewan again led the way when it extended its hospital insurance plan to cover medical services received outside hospitals. In 1968, the federal government offered to cost-share all qualifying medical services. By 1972, all provinces and territories had converted their hospital insurance plans to comprehensive public health insurance plans. (We will come back later to the importance of this pattern of innovation by one province, followed by efforts by the federal government to spread the benefits of this innovation to the whole country.)

It is important to recognize that the officials who managed the introduction of public hospital insurance in the late 1950s and public health insurance in the late 1960s took great pains to design a system that would avoid the problems they saw in both Great Britain and the United States. Many saw the British experiment with socialized medicine as seriously flawed, and the American approach as too heartless. The Canadian solution was a hybrid system. Hospitals would continue to operate at arm's length from the government, under the direction of their boards of trustees. Unlike in Britain, doctors would remain private practitioners, and would not become employees of the state. However, Canadian hospitals and doctors would both be funded through a publicly administered and publicly financed health insurance program.

Canada's health insurance system is frequently attacked by people who argue that it is open to abuse by both patients and doctors. Within certain limits, this is true. The architects of the system deliberately chose to build into it what they believed were essential freedoms. These include the freedom for citizens to choose their own doctor and the freedom of doctors to prescribe what they believe to be the best treatment in the circumstances. A small minority of citizens and physicians abuse these freedoms. However, this is a trivial price to pay for a system that has huge advantages over the alternatives.

Some of these same critics argue in favour of user fees, or favour a two-tier system, whereby the wealthy can buy services without having to wait their turn behind other Canadians. What these critics fail to recognize are the enormous strengths of the existing Canadian system.

First, the Canadian single-payer health insurance plan is systemically more efficient than the U.S. system of private health insurance. Many people erroneously assume that publicly administered services always cost more than they would if they were provided by the "efficient" private sector. The U.S. system of thousands of private sector insurers, however, is systemically inefficient. Each of those companies has a senior management team, an accounting system, an advertising budget, and on top of everything else, wants to make a profit for the shareholders. This is duplication of effort on a massive scale, and it costs U.S. citizens tens of billions of unnecessary dollars.

This issue was studied in depth by the U.S. Office of Technology Assessment during President Bill Clinton's abortive effort to reform the U.S. health insurance system in the early 1990s. Until it was eliminated in one of the Republican Congress's budget cuts, the OTA was regarded by most knowledgeable observers as the best public policy research agency in the world. In 1994, the OTA published a study entitled *International Comparisons of Administrative Costs in Health Care*. Using 1991 as the base year, the OTA compared the costs of administering health services in Canada and the U.S. The OTA estimated that if the U.S. had a single-payer system like Canada's, it would have saved somewhere between $47 billion and $98 billion (U.S.) in 1991. This is the equivalent of 6 to 13 percent of the total U.S. health expenditure for that year. Depending on the estimate, the savings the U.S. could have realized by adopting the Canadian system are at the low end almost as much as or at the high end much more than the entire Canadian health care budget, which in 1991 was $66 billion in *Canadian* dollars.

The United States has the most expensive health care system in the world, both absolutely and in relative terms. In 1992, the U.S. spent 14.1 percent of its economic output on health care. The U.S. Congressional Budget Office estimated that given present trends, U.S. health care expenditures would reach 18 percent of GNP by the year 2000 — a whopping $1.7 trillion! In 1992, approximately half of U.S. health costs were paid by governments (federal, state, and local), and the other half by private citizens and health insurers.

Despite spending the most on health care, the U.S. does not have the best health outcomes in the world. As the OTA notes in a 1993 report entitled *International Health Statistics: What the Numbers Mean for the United States*, "The United States spends a higher proportion of its national income on health care than any of its peers in the international community and yet continually ranks poorly in *some* key areas of health. Death rates for infants, children, and young and middle-aged adults, for example, are substantially higher than in other industrialized countries."

By contrast, Canada's total health expenditures are roughly 9.2 percent of our economic output, and the trend is down — health expenditures peaked in 1992 at 10.2 percent of GDP. At that time, approximately 75 percent of this was paid by governments. Unlike in the U.S., all Canadians are covered by public health insurance, and hence have full access to the health care system. Clearly, Canadians are getting a better deal.

This brings us to the second major advantage of the Canadian system. Because most health expenditures are made through government, governments have the ability to exercise considerable, although not total, control over the system. While maintaining the privacy of individual medical records, government agencies monitor medical services on a regional basis, looking for discrepancies that might justify some sort of intervention. For example, a few years ago monitoring revealed that one particular region in Ontario had a rate of Caesarean births that was twice the national average. On investigation, it was discovered that this was the result of a lack of training on the part of the physicians in the region. When this deficiency was addressed, the C-section rate went down to the national average, which was obviously to the benefit of the mothers and babies concerned, as well as the taxpayers.

This example illustrates one of the crucial myths about the public sector that partly inspired this book. Many of the advocates of downsizing and privatization in the public service argue that this will benefit taxpayers because the cost to government will be reduced. Typically, however, these advocates look narrowly at the cost to government and fail to consider the impact on the costs to society as a whole.

The health care systems in Canada and the U.S. offer a classic example of the difference between the cost to governments and the cost to society. Health care costs paid by governments in the U.S. are proportionately far less than health care costs paid by governments in Canada. But the cost of health care to U.S. society as a whole is proportionately far more than the cost to Canadian society — and will soon be almost twice as much if present trends continue.

The reason U.S. society pays more for health care is not because, as some economists argue, Americans *prefer* to spend more of their income in this way. It is because neither the U.S. government nor its citizens have the ability to exercise any substantive control over more than half of the health care system. In Canada, governments pay a higher share, but as citizens we pay less overall. This is an important lesson to keep in mind. While there is often room for prudent budget-cutting in the public sector, we need to make sure that those who would cut health, education, and social welfare do not end up raising the costs of these services to Canadian society as a whole. It is worrying that the current trend is towards increasing private health expenditure.

The third major benefit of the Canadian system is that it creates a competitive advantage for the Canadian economy. Take the automotive industry, for example. With a population that is about 10 percent of that in the U.S., Canada assembles about 20 percent of the cars in North America. Why would U.S. executives decide to make Canada home to twice as much production capacity as is necessary to serve the Canadian market? The fact is that Canada is more competitive than the U.S. in this sector, and lower health insurance costs are a significant factor in this competitiveness.

Looking back, we can see that the implementation of public hospital insurance in the late 1950s and early 1960s created the context for the subsequent massive expansion of hospitals, clinics, medical training facilities, and all the other components of our health care system. Using Ontario as an example, this can be illustrated by the early reports of the Ontario Hospital Services Commission, which was the agency that oversaw the introduction of the Ontario Hospital Insurance Plan on January 1, 1959.

Prior to the advent of hospital insurance, the health care system in Ontario was a patchwork quilt of private medical practitioners, private clinics, and community hospitals funded through philanthropy or run by religious orders. In the first few years of the operation of the Hospital Insurance Plan, payments to hospitals for insured services in Ontario rose from $155 million in 1959 to $215 million in 1961. However, in the course of administering the insurance plan, the Ontario Hospital Services Commission quickly recognized the need to involve itself in a host of matters related to the overall efficiency of the hospital system. These included ensuring that enough beds existed across the province and regionally to meet demand; creating a special capital subsidy to enable hospitals with substandard facilities to upgrade them; encouraging the expansion and improvement of training facilities for nurses; coordinating the development of a uniform pension plan for hospital staff, to be administered through the Ontario Hospital Association; examining the budgets of all hospitals and establishing appropriate rates for reimbursement; coordinating the development of shared laundry facilities for hospitals in the Toronto core; and beginning the collection of statistical data to support decision-making about the operation of the system as a whole.

Public health insurance was the catalyst that got the Ontario government (and the other provincial governments as well) directly involved in the provision of health services. It led to the application of what were then considered modern management and public administration techniques to a sector in which these techniques had never been brought to bear. Once started down this road, there was no turning back.

The Canadian health insurance system is not perfect, nor is the health care system as a whole. There are many improvements that can and should be made. However, Canadians owe a great deal to those individuals who took part in the great National Project of the 1940s, 1950s, and 1960s to build Canada's public health insurance system and expand health care services. With the benefit of hindsight, we can see that the decision to make insurance public while leaving hospitals and doctors to continue as independent, private actors within the overall health system was an inspired one. We have so far avoided many of the problems experienced in the U.K., while still enjoying the efficiency of a single-payer, public health insurance system.

Public health insurance is a classic example of John Ralston Saul's arguments, as outlined above. We chose to limit the ability of the wealthy to get preferential access to medical services in order to provide equitable access for all Canadians. Conrad Black to the contrary, this innovation is one of the important ingredients in the Canada We Have, and one we want to keep.

EDUCATION FOR ALL

At the beginning of the 1950s, Canada's educational system was designed to meet the basic requirements of a population made up largely of manual labourers. Fewer than 40 percent of Canadians finished high school. Only about 5 percent went on to post-secondary education.

Fifty years later, Canada leads the world in educational attainment as measured by the U.N.'s Human Development Index, which combines adult literacy and primary, secondary, and tertiary enrolment. Almost 70 percent of those between the ages of five and twenty-nine are enrolled in some sort of formal education. This transformation illustrates the success of the second great National Project of the post-war era — making it possible for the majority of Canadians to enjoy the benefits of a good education.

Canada's National Project in education effectively began in 1952, when the federal government introduced a system of per capita grants for post-secondary education. In the late 1940s, universities in Canada were in a fiscal crisis. Enrolments had skyrocketed when veterans returned from the Second World War, and provincial funding had not kept up with demand.

However, a far more pressing requirement was to expand Canada's educational system to cope with the Baby Boom. In the decade from 1946 to 1955, 3.9 million Canadians were born — 50 percent more than had been born in the previous ten-year period. The number of Canadians aged fifteen to nineteen doubled between 1951 and 1971. Accommodating these Baby Boomers required successive waves of school construction — elementary schools in the 1950s, high schools in the 1960s, and universities and community colleges in the late 1960s and 1970s.

Education is a provincial responsibility under the constitution, and the costs of building and staffing these new schools soon began to take their toll on all provinces, especially the poorer ones. Under the federal-provincial fiscal arrangements of the time, most of the taxing power was controlled by the federal government, but the provinces were faced with rising education, health, road construction, and energy costs. It was clear that some sort of fiscal accommodation was required.

The solution was equalization, which was introduced in 1957. The principles underlying it were enunciated much earlier, in the 1940 report of the Royal Commission on Dominion-Provincial Relations, commonly known as the Rowell-Sirois report. The commission recommended that Canada establish a national system of adjustment grants. The grants should be designed "to make it possible for every province to provide, for its people, services of average Canadian standards and they will thus alleviate distress and shameful conditions which now weaken national unity and handicap many Canadians. They are the concrete expression of the Commission's conception of a federal system which will both preserve a healthy local autonomy and build a stronger and more united nation."

Equalization grants compensated the poorer provinces for their lack of revenue-generating capacity, and made it possible for them to offer comparable services without having to impose higher-than-average taxes. Equalization grants were not specific to education — they were, and still are, provided without strings attached — but the need for adequate educational standards across the country was one of the key reasons they were introduced.

Pressure on the post-secondary system increased as the Baby Boomers graduated from high school. In 1967, the federal government introduced a shared-cost program, under which it agreed to fund 50 percent of the operating costs of post-secondary education. In 1977, this program was rolled into the Established Programs Financing Grant, which provided lump-sum payments to provinces to help fund health, education, and social services.

In addition to their own funding, the provinces helped make post-secondary education more accessible by limiting tuition fees to approximately 15 percent of the total cost, and by creating a system of community and technical colleges to provide an alternative form of post-secondary training. In 1964, the federal government created the Canada Student Loans program, designed to help make post-secondary education more accessible for students from lower-income families.

It must be admitted that increased accessibility wasn't the only reason for the rapid increase in educational levels among Canadians. Continuing high youth unemployment was undoubtedly a factor. Many students concluded that because jobs were not available, they might as well stay in school in the hopes of getting a better job later on. For most, this proved to be a blessing in disguise.

Like the health care system, Canada's education system has many shortcomings and flaws. The post-secondary educational system developed in Canada in the post-war era reflects the compromises described by Saul. Rather than focusing on providing the best possible education to the minority, Canada chose to focus on providing a decent education to the majority. Many argue that in making this choice, academic standards suffered and too much emphasis was placed on the utilitarian aspects of education and training.

However, it is evident from the United Nation's indicators that the current generation of Canadian youth has clearly got the message about the benefits of a good education, and is taking full advantage of an educational system that was established in its current form largely in the 1950s, 1960s, and 1970s.

INCOME SECURITY FOR ALL

The Great Depression of the 1930s convinced many Canadians that an appropriate role for the state was to use the power of the collective to alleviate the suffering of individuals. The principles underlying a new approach to income security were first described in a 1943 report prepared by social scientist Leonard Marsh. Central to his *Report on Social Security for Canada* was the concept of social insurance.

Previously, Canadians in need were helped through social relief payments or charity. The concept of social insurance involves creating a pool of funds through taxation or mandatory contributions, and using these funds to protect the income of Canadians from risks such as sickness, old age, disability, and unemployment. According to Marsh, "The genius of social insurance is that it enlists the direct support of the classes most likely to benefit, and enlists equally the participation and controlling influence of the state, at the same time as it avoids the evil of pauperization, and the undemocratic influence of excessive state philanthropy."

In accordance with this concept, the federal government, in most cases with the collaboration of the provincial governments, introduced or modified a series of social programs: unemployment insurance was introduced in 1940, but substantially revised in 1955; family allowance appeared in 1944; old age security in 1951; federal support for social assistance through the Canada Assistance Plan in 1964; the Canada Pension Plan in 1965; spouse's allowance in 1975; and the Child Tax Credit in 1978.

Some of these programs are more "insurance-like" (i.e., based on the payment of premiums), while others are universal entitlements funded from general government revenues and still others use the tax system to provide benefits. In combination, they create Canada's "social safety net," which is designed to reduce inequality and ensure a minimum standard of income security for all Canadians.

While most Canadians support the principles underlying income security, many blame these social programs for the fiscal deficits that started to emerge in the mid-1970s, and got larger and larger through the 1980s and early 1990s. There is room for debate about the degree to which Canada's deficits were the result of failing to protect the revenue base in the face of structural adjustment, rather than the result of overspending on social programs. However, there is no doubt that there were significant problems with the design and implementation of some of these programs.

In some cases, they seem to have prolonged dependence rather than created incentives to regain self-sufficiency. Critics noted that similar social programs in Scandinavia allocated more resources to active adjustment than to passive income support.

The federal government can be justly criticized for failing to adjust the Unemployment Insurance program to take account of new realities. From the 1970s on, the major cause of unemployment was not periodic down-turns in the business cycle, but a profound structural change in the economy. By the time this became more generally understood, those dependent on the existing system had become so entrenched that it was virtually impossible to redesign the system to support active structural adjustment rather than passive income support.

As foreseen by Leonard Marsh, avoiding both the evil of pauperization and the undemocratic influence of excessive state philanthropy requires what Saul would call a continuous "act of reconciliation." The broad vision of social insurance is, nevertheless, embedded in Canadian society. Conrad Black may criticize this as a convoy proceeding at the pace of the slowest ship, but he might well remind himself of the purpose of a convoy in the first place.

HUMAN RIGHTS FOR ALL

Another major achievement of the post-war era was a significant strength-ening of human rights for all Canadians. In the aftermath of the Second World War, Canadians became aware of the reduction in civil liberties that had accompanied the war effort. Many were ashamed of the treatment accorded Japanese-Canadians who were interned during the war. Canada was active in supporting the creation of the United Nations, in part to strengthen civil liberties internationally, and it was logical that this issue should receive domestic attention as well.

John Diefenbaker spoke on human rights regularly in the House of Commons beginning in 1945, and campaigned in 1957 and 1958 on a promise to introduce the Canadian Bill of Rights, which he did in 1960. In 1960, Canada also gave up the shameful practice of denying the vote to aboriginal Canadians living on reserves.

In 1967, Lester Pearson established a Royal Commission on the Status of Women in Canada, signalling the federal government's recognition that many women were denied full participation in Canadian society on the grounds of gender alone, and that a major process of societal change was necessary.

Pierre Trudeau came to Canadian politics with one overriding objective: to make it impossible for there to be another government in Canada like that of Maurice Duplessis in Quebec — intolerant, discriminatory, and totalitarian. Trudeau's career in Canadian politics was capped in 1982 by the entrenchment in the Canadian constitution of the Charter of Rights and Freedoms. Along the way, Trudeau also made bilingualism a cornerstone of the federal government; provided funding for aboriginal groups, which was a critical factor in the subsequent emergence of aboriginal leaders on the national political scene; recognized the contribution to Canadian society of immigrants through a policy on multiculturalism in 1971; and strengthened human rights in 1977 with the adoption of the Canadian Human Rights Act and the subsequent establishment of the Canadian Human Rights Commission.

Seeking the right balance between fundamental freedoms, democratic rights, mobility rights, legal rights, equality rights, and language rights, within the reasonable limits that can be demonstrably justified in a free and democratic society, is a journey that is never over. Subsequent initiatives have focused on preventing discrimination based on sexual orientation, improving gender equity, and attempting to redress the injustices suffered by Canada's aboriginal peoples. The accomplishments of the 1960–82 period represented enormous progress, and Canadians are justifiably proud that they live in a society widely recognized as one of the most open and tolerant in the world.

CANADIAN CULTURE

The single most important event in the development of Canadian culture, prior to the emergence of the Internet, was the report of the Royal Commission on National Development in the Arts, Letters and Sciences, commonly referred to as the Massey-Lévesque Commission. The commission's report, published in 1951, laid the groundwork for the astonishingly successful National Project on Canadian culture that took place in the 1950s, 1960s, and 1970s.

This National Project cannot take credit for the existence of Canadians with literary, artistic, musical, intellectual, or dramatic talents. But it can take credit for creating better opportunities for those talents to be recognized, developed, and rewarded.

It is worth reminding ourselves that, with respect to our intellectual and cultural life, Canada's circumstances are unique in the world. Here is how the Massey-Lévesque Commission described them:

Canadians, with their customary optimism, may think that the fate of their civilization is in their own hands. So it is. But this young nation, struggling to be itself, must shape its course with an eye to three conditions so familiar that their significance can too easily be ignored. Canada has a small and scattered population in a vast area; this population is clustered along the rim of another country many times more populous and of far greater economic strength; a majority of Canadians share their mother tongue with that neighbour, which leads to peculiarly close and intimate relations. One or two of these conditions will be found in many modern countries. But Canada alone possesses all three.

The Massey-Lévesque Commission convinced a generation of Canadians that given these unique circumstances, the federal government had two fundamental responsibilities with respect to the intellectual and cultural life of the country: first, to ensure that Canadians engaged in the arts and research could earn a decent living; and second, to ensure that their efforts would not simply be drowned out by competition from across the U.S. border.

Over the next three decades, the federal government introduced a series of measures in keeping with the spirit of the Massey-Lévesque Commission's vision. The establishment of the Canada Council in March 1957 provided a mechanism to enable direct funding for writers, artists, and other participants in the creative arts. Over the years, this has been supplemented by industrial and institutional support programs directed at publishing, film, television, museums, galleries, music, dance, and theatre.

The federal government also gradually introduced funding mechanisms to support university-based research, leading eventually to the establishment of the three major funding councils — the Medical Research Council, the Natural Sciences and Engineering Research Council, and the Social Sciences and Humanities Research Council. Almost every university researcher in Canada today will be supported at some stage in his or her career by MRC, NSERC, or SSHRC grants.

The Massey-Lévesque Commission also reinforced the need for federal regulations to ensure Canadian content in publishing, on the radio, and on the emerging new medium of the time, television. Hundreds of thousands of actors, directors, singers, musicians, camera operators, and technicians owe their success to regulations that require radio and television stations to broadcast a minimum amount of Canadian-produced programming. In the absence of such regulations, private sector broadcasters would clearly have purchased most of their content from across the border. It has always been cheaper to buy the rights to rebroadcast a U.S. show than to produce one in Canada.

Similarly, thousands of Canadian writers and editors owe their success to grants to authors and publishers, postal subsidies, cross-border advertising restrictions, and ownership regulations that ensured that Canadians would have access to books and magazines published in Canada, in addition to those imported from the U.S.

The result is that for the past three decades in particular, Canadians have had the best of both worlds. We have a thriving music industry, a film and video industry that rivals that of New York (which is second only to Hollywood in North America), leading-edge entertainment software companies like Alias, SoftImage, Discreet Logic, and a plethora of award-winning authors who are recognized throughout the world. At the same time, we have complete access to U.S. culture: Hollywood movies dominate Canadian cinema screens and video-rental outlets; more than 80 percent of publications on the newsstands are from the U.S.; all the U.S. best-sellers are displayed in Canadian bookstores; all the best (and worst) U.S. music is rebroadcast on Canadian radio stations; and all the best (and worst) U.S. television shows are available on satellite, by cable, and over the air.

Canadian content regulations (which some regard as a misnomer, because they don't really refer to content but to the nationality of those involved in the production) were never designed to censor or prevent access to U.S. content. Rather, they were intended to ensure that our citizens would have access to both Canadian and U.S. content. Only in this way could Canadians create "a coalition of ideas based on an assumption of the public good."

PHYSICAL INFRASTRUCTURE

A large part of today's economy is running on infrastructure that was initially built in the 1950s. During this decade, there was an enormous increase in the transportation network all across the country. The Trans-Canada Highway — the first road linking all provinces of Canada — was opened in 1962. The St. Lawrence Seaway was started in 1954 and, incredible at it seems, completed less than five years later, in April 1959. For the first time, it was possible for ocean-going ships to call at ports throughout the Great Lakes.

Also in the 1950s, airports were constructed in major cities throughout the country to accommodate the new passenger aircraft that were revolutionizing business and personal travel. Similarly, phone lines and microwave networks were built to serve the huge growth in personal and business communications.

Beginning in 1955, oil and, later, gas pipelines were built to deliver energy to markets in Eastern Canada, British Columbia, and the United States. The National Energy Board was created in 1959 to oversee the construction and management of the pipeline network.

In Ontario alone, more than forty generating facilities were brought on-line between 1945 and 1972, expanding Ontario Hydro's generation capacity to thirteen million kilowatts, six times what it had been in 1945. Most of the locations in the province that were suitable for large water-generator facilities were taken up by the end of the 1950s, leading Ontario Hydro to shift its emphasis to thermal and, later, nuclear power. In the early 1950s, Ontario Hydro changed motors in seven million appliances in one million homes, preparing for the shift to a sixty-cycle alternating current, which had been adopted as the standard in North America. These initiatives were mirrored across Canada.

Of course, similar development of physical infrastructure took place during this period in the U.S. and parts of Europe and Asia. What is unique about Canada is not the physical infrastructure we built, but rather the social infrastructure resulting from the other five National Projects of the post-war era.

One final but crucial point in this brief historical excursion. Canada's National Projects of the 1950s, 1960s, and 1970s were accomplished largely without budget deficits. The federal and provincial governments did not start running regular deficits until the late 1970s, and it was not until the 1980s that they ballooned into the chronic problem that was not resolved until the late 1990s.

WHAT HAPPENED TO NATIONAL PROJECTS?

Canadians know better than anyone that these National Projects have been fraught with the normal problems of delay, wrong turnings, bureaucracy, waste, and other human failings. As a result, Canadians find it hard to rejoice whole-heartedly at the fact that our society has reached the top of the league tables, according to the United Nations. We'll throw a party if we win the gold medal in hockey, but not, apparently, if we win the gold medal for having the best society.

Part of this diffidence is due to the fact that many of us have forgotten how we got here. The National Projects of the 1950s, 1960s, and early 1970s have been overshadowed by our more recent history. When we look back over the most recent twenty-five years, what do we see? There are no new major National Projects — only a continuation of the ones launched earlier. In the 1980s and 1990s, the big issues were the deficit, unemployment, the Goods and Services Tax, and free trade. And of course, national unity, where we can look back fondly on the failure of the Meech Lake and Charlottetown accords.

This is the picture of government that is uppermost in the minds of Canadians who came of age in the 1970s and later. And a depressing picture it is. Instead of focusing on the vision, we've been rummaging around in the plumbing.No wonder younger Canadians tend to be cynical about the ability of government to carry out major under-takings. It doesn't help that under fiscal pressure, some governments have been tempted to unravel part of what was accomplished by these National Projects.

In 1998, for the first time, the United Nations included a Human Poverty Index with the Human Development Index. Here, Canada did not fare so well, ranking only eighth out of seventeen industrial countries. More worrisome is the fact that the 1998 Human Development Index rankings were based on 1995 data, which means that the consequences of many of the cuts to social programs brought in by the 1995 federal budget, combined with concurrent cuts in provincial social budgets, will not begin to be seen until later data is compiled by the U.N.

Former federal bureaucrat Arthur Kroeger refers to the 1995 budget as a "book-end" marking the close of an era of activist, interventionist federal government that began at the end of the Second World War. The 1995 federal budget implemented the results of Program Review, a process for reducing the budgets and programs of almost all federal departments.

Program Review was clearly necessary to reduce intolerably large annual federal deficits. But not all government programs, particularly in the social welfare field, were wasteful, and over time we may come to regret the impact of some of these cuts on Canada's human development.

In the 1990s, we began to see a breakdown of the political consensus that supported National Projects through the 1950s, 1960s, 1970s, and into the 1980s. It is remarkable that during this period, Canada's National Projects were largely above partisan politics. Of course, there was plenty of disagreement about the means to accomplish them, but generally there was profound agreement about the objectives. All six major National Projects carried on despite changes in government at both the federal and provincial levels. New Democrats, Liberals, and Progressive Conservatives shared the same broad vision. The competition was less about the vision than about who could best accomplish it.

It is not at all clear today to what degree the members of the Reform Party, and their regressive conservative fellow travellers, embrace the vision underlying Canada's National Projects of the 1950s, 1960s, and 1970s. And of course, the Bloc Québécois has an entirely different agenda.

QUEBEC'S NATIONAL PROJECT

Although National Projects have been missing from the Canadian scene since the mid-1970s, they were alive and well in Quebec.

It was good news for both Canada and Quebec that in the 1960s and 1970s, a cadre of leaders emerged, determined to transform Quebec society. The bad news was that there was profound disagreement among these leaders as to whether the result of this transformation should be a revitalized Quebec within the existing Canadian federation or a new sovereign state.

While there was disagreement about the ultimate objective, however, there was a strong consensus that actions should be taken to strengthen the province economically, culturally, and socially. This was the aim of

Quebec's National Project, or *projet de société*. Quebec's National Project was effectively launched in 1962, when the Quebec Liberals fought and won the provincial election with a promise to nationalize the hydro-electric energy system. It fell to René Lévesque, as natural resources minister, to implement this promise. Since that time, Hydro-Québec has been used, more or less efficiently, as an engine for developing the technical capabilities of a significant component of Quebec's private sector, through, for example, the rise of global engineering giants such as SNC-Lavalin.

The second major initiative was to set up pools of capital that could be used to foster the development of francophone entrepreneurs. When Jacques Parizeau, then an economic adviser to Premier Jean Lesage, heard about proposals to create the Canada Pension Plan, he realized this was an opportunity for Quebec to amass the capital needed to invest in Quebec-based businesses. Rather than going along with the federal plan, the province set up its own pension plan in 1965, along with a new institution — the Caisse de dépôt et placement du Québec — to manage the investments. In this respect, Quebec was smarter than Ottawa. As originally designed, the Canada Pension Plan did not create a pool of capital — rather, the contributions collected from Canadians were included in the general revenues of the federal government. Quebec went one better and accumulated these contributions to create an enormous pool of capital, which gave it the ability to chart its own economic course.

When René Lévesque became premier in 1976, with Jacques Parizeau as his finance minister, Quebec's National Project moved into high gear. The immediate objective was to transform the Quebec economy into one dominated by successful francophone entrepreneurs, rather than the anglophone enterprises of the past. Crown corporations were set up in various sectors, the Quebec Stock Savings Plan was established, francophone business schools were created or expanded, and the financial industry in Quebec was deregulated. The result was that during the 1980s, Quebec's francophone businesses thrived. Taking advantage of the mechanisms established to protect Canadian culture generally, its franco-phone cultural industries also flourished. As anticipated by Lévesque, although he did not live to see it, the resulting burst of confidence and pride among Quebecers has helped perpetuate the sovereignty movement.

The vision underlying Quebec's National Project was a powerful one. Faced with the dearth of vision in the rest of Canada, is it any wonder that successive generations of young francophones were captivated by it? In the 1980s and early 1990s, it seemed to Quebecers that Canada had lost its way. Quebec, by contrast, had what appeared to be a working strategy for creating the economic instruments that would enable its citizens to be *maîtres chez nous*. If Ottawa didn't know what to do with its constitutional powers, Quebecers felt they could use them more effectively. Of course, provincial politicians always want more power, but in this instance, Quebec's leaders believed recent experience supported the idea that the provincial government could do more to build Quebec's economy than Ottawa. To get these additional powers, Quebec needed a new deal with the rest of Canada. This was essentially the argument of the Allaire report.

By the mid-1990s, Quebec's National Project started running out of steam, dragged down by provincial government deficits, too many bad investments by provincial agencies, and the continuing economic uncertainty created by the sovereignists. But Quebecers remember the collective pride and enthusiasm of earlier days, and long for it to be rekindled.

Like most Canadians, Quebecers take it for granted that they live in a society where access to health care and education is a basic right, where a social safety net ensures a minimum level of income security, and where human rights are protected and gradually enhanced. Naturally, most are more familiar with francophone Quebec culture than anglophone Canadian culture. Like most Canadians, Quebecers have forgotten how much is owed to the generation that launched the National Projects that created the Canada We Have.

4

Me versus Us

In 1993, in its famous Red Book, the Liberal Party of Canada said that the coming election was about one simple question: "What kind of a country do we want for ourselves and our children?" That is also the central question for this book. In answering that question, the Red Book said, in part:

> We want a country where all of us see ourselves as contributors and participants, not liabilities and dependants. . . .
>
> We want a country that realizes the value of community. In an age of globalization, we want to belong to a national community that feels distinctively ours. We want to support our local communities as the source of our social stability and economic strength. . . .
>
> We want a country whose governments are efficient, innovative, and cooperative not only with each other but with business, labour, the learning sector, environmentalists, and volunteer groups.

We want, in short, to see ourselves as winners, as a country that solves problems, a country that works, and in doing so serves as a model for other countries around the world.

This was clearly a very different vision of Canada than the one that is held by Conrad Black and implied in the writings of William Gibson and Ian Angell, but by what method was this vision to be achieved?

The Red Book answered, "We believe that if Canada is to work as a country, Canadians have to see themselves as belonging not to a society composed of isolated individuals or of competing interest groups, but to a society of reciprocal obligation, in which each of us is responsible for the well-being of the other. Canadians know this intuitively. We take pride in a health care system that is there for all of us, not just for me."

A health care system for all of us, not just for me: these simple words express both a value system and a complex moral choice that Canadians have chosen to make explicit. Of course, in moments of crisis, all of us want the best medical care for our families and loved ones — we would be less than human if we did not — but as a society, confronted with choosing either a health care system that is accessible to all or a system where the quality of care is dependent on a person's ability to pay, Canadians have opted for a system that benefits everyone equally.

We make this choice because we have become a society that would be ashamed of tolerating a situation, as Americans do daily, in which forty million of our fellow citizens go without any form of medical protection. Canadians (and most Europeans) have come to see universal health care as an essential and fundamental attribute of civic society, indeed of civilization itself. We are not able to avert our eyes from the plight of our fellow citizens, a feat of mental and moral gymnastics that millions of Americans seem blithely able to perform, apparently without the slightest twinge of conscience.

And yet it was not always thus in Canada. As we noted in Chapter 3, before the introduction of hospital insurance, we lived with a medical care system that closely resembled that of the Americans. Indeed, this sense of "us" as expressed through the morality of public health insurance is a relatively new phenomenon. Previously, we eased our consciences by relying on doctors to take on so-called charity cases for free. Like contemporary Americans, we chose not to ask ourselves whether it was possible that some people were falling through the cracks. We never viewed medical care as a "system" that should be accessible to all; we saw the world only through the lens of individual, rather than societal, obligation.

So what produced this fundamental shift in our attitude towards health care? In Canada, it began with the visionary political leadership of the Co-operative Commonwealth Federation (CCF) and Tommy Douglas in Saskatchewan, leadership that was undergirded by Prairie populism and a religious commitment to the betterment of humankind. The cause was then taken up by the federal government, and public health insurance gradually became a national reality and a national value. But the point has to be underlined: it was the vision, idealism, leadership, and policy of a generation of federal and provincial politicians that produced this major refinement of the definition of what it means to be a Canadian.

The morality underlying public health insurance illustrates the larger choices we must make as we face the new millennium. This is a discussion about what we owe each other as fellow citizens not only of Canada but also of the world. To what extent should we see ourselves as "members one of another," in the words of St. Paul to the Ephesians? What do we really mean by the term "national community"? Are these values outmoded, inappropriate, ineffectual in the face of the pressures of globalization? Can they constitute more than a moral response, more than a hopeless, futile, nostalgic, chivalrous gesture in confronting the gospels according to Conrad Black, Ian Angell, and William Gibson?

As John Ralston Saul reminds us, however, this communitarian, collectivist, humanitarian impulse is historically rooted in practical necessity. In a poor country and harsh climate, we must hang together or we shall assuredly hang separately. The need to work together, to look out for each other, goes beyond charity and decency. It began with the stark realities of survival. In its origins, this was a highly pragmatic morality.

Is this still the case today? It is our contention that in the face of global challenges, the societal imperative is more necessary than ever, not simply because it is the right thing to do (though it is), not merely because it is in the great historical tradition of Canada, but because our future survival as a country demands it. To think and act as a society is what "real countries" do. Thinking societally is a strategy — is, indeed, the only strategy — with which to counter the globalizers.

To argue for society is, of course, to place ourselves on a collision course with the dominant ideology of the day, which centres on a fundamental belief in two related tenets: unbridled individualism and free markets. Sylvia Ostry, Canada's eminent international trade theorist and practitioner, has dubbed this belief structure "Ronald Thatcherism," in honour of its two leading exponents in the 1980s. It was Prime Minister Margaret Thatcher, after all, who coined the memorable aphorism "There is no such thing as society, only individuals and their families." Former U.S. labour secretary Robert Reich less politely refers to this way of thinking as "brutish market triumphalism."

The crisis of the international markets in 1998 has forced a radical re-evaluation of hitherto unquestioned assumptions about the inevitable world triumph of capitalism through free markets. The last gasp of the Old World may have been taken at the World Economic Forum in Davos, Switzerland, in the winter of 1998. Two thousand of the world's leading business people and politicians gathered for their annual get-together, consuming in the process, as the *Financial Times* of London put it, "roughly 70% of the world's daily output of self-congratulation."

Lewis Lapham, the editor of *Harper's*, attended the event and described the intervention of George Soros, the extraordinarily successful American businessman who made $1 billion (U.S.) in the fall of 1992 betting against the value of the British pound on world currency markets. Soros's warnings in February 1998 sound amazingly prescient in light of subsequent events. Only fools believe in the conscience of markets, Soros said — fools and tenured professors of economics. Markets are as dumb as posts and as blind as bats; they're inherently unstable because they are dependent on what people wish for, not what they have in hand, and therefore are impossible to maintain in a state of equilibrium.

"Imagine a pendulum," Soros explained, "a pendulum that has become a wrecking ball, swinging out of control and with increasing speed, knocking over one economy after another. First Mexico, then Indonesia and South Korea, and who knows what happens next? Maybe Brazil. Maybe Japan. . . . Market fundamentalism doesn't work. Without the intervention in Asia of the IMF [International Monetary Fund] and the World Bank, the whole system would have fallen apart." Left to its own devices, he said, the global market undoubtedly would destroy itself, though not for any ideological reason (not because it hated rich people or neglected to vote Republican, say), but because it obeyed the laws of motion rather than the laws of reason, and hence didn't know how to do anything else except destroy itself.

It would be foolish to frame this debate in terms of absolute choices (i.e., either individualism and free markets or community and society). John Ralston Saul had it right: Canadians have traditionally sought a balance between individual and collective rights. To argue for community and society, to argue for the importance of the nation and its National Projects, is not to reject the importance of individualism and markets, but is merely to place them in their proper perspective. As Mackenzie King might have put it, "Markets if necessary, but not necessarily markets."

All we are arguing is that individualism and markets ought not to be absolute and supreme in our hierarchy of national values.

THE THIRD WAY AND ITS ORIGINS

Some have called this approach the Third Way, a view which will seem so comfortable and familiar to us as Canadians that the more we hear of it, the more we may think we invented it. Indeed, the passages quoted at the beginning of this chapter from the Liberals' 1993 Red Book may confirm Canada as one of the earliest, if unwitting, heralds of the Third Way.

The essential principle of the Third Way is the explicit rejection of the extremes of traditional left and right political positions in favour of a middle way. Revealingly, the most enthusiastic current proponents of this philosophy can be found in Britain and the United States, where Margaret Thatcher and Ronald Reagan used to reign supreme. Those who support the Third Way, most notably Britain's "New Labour" prime minister, Tony Blair, but also Bill Clinton in the United States, accept both the crucial role of markets and the need for the elimination of trade and investment barriers internationally. But they also see national governments taking an active role in ensuring social investments in education and in helping individuals cope with the adjustment to the new economy. One of Blair's chief advisers, Anthony Giddens, director of the London School of Economics and author of *The Third Way*, says the purpose of the movement is "saving capitalism from itself by humanizing it."

A central tenet of the doctrine of the Third Way is the rejection of Ian Angell's division of the globalized world into winners and losers. Tony Blair stresses not only the virtue but also the utility of social inclusion, with the state preparing everyone, through education and training, for success in the economy, rather than simply letting the market determine our fate.

British economic and social analyst David Marquand also describes the dangers of increasing the divisions between global winners and losers. Like Angell, he says the biggest share of global productivity gains has gone to "the owners of capital, to a new techno-managerial elite and to a handful of stars in the increasingly global entertainment industries." But he warns, "They are increasingly detached from the community and nation, and increasingly unwilling to pay their share of the social costs which the new capitalism has brought in its train. They want to hang onto their winnings and they also want to maintain a global economic system in which they can win even more."

The losers in this scenario are the insecure middle classes, with their frozen pay cheques and threatened jobs, contract and part-time workers, and ever larger numbers of their rank who are outside the economy altogether. In rejecting Angell's enthusiastic embrace of this divided world, Marquand points out that "no project of social inclusion will work unless it captures some of the winners' gains and redirects them to the losers."

David Crane of the *Toronto Star*, commenting on Marquand, notes, "It is an illusion to believe that governments can, as the 'Third Way' tries to have it, provide improved education and training, make investments in early childhood development, strengthen social support systems and sustain health care at zero cost." Translation: There is no getting around the winners' paying their fair share of taxes if we are going to live in a just and equitable society.

Still, the Third Way continues to find new adherents. In the face of the continuing world financial crisis, there are signs that even the most orthodox of international institutions is changing its thinking on the sanctity of markets. In October 1998, the World Bank in Washington issued its *World Development Report* for that year. "Recent development thinking has been based on the assumption that markets work well enough to ensure development and alleviate poverty," read the report. "Our growing understanding of information constraints suggests that markets alone are not adequate; societies also require institutions to facilitate the acquisition, adaptation and dissemination of knowledge, and to mitigate information failures, especially as they affect the poor."

This shift in thinking can be attributed, in part, to the role that American Joseph Stiglitz, former chairman of Bill Clinton's Council of Economic Advisors and now chief economist of the World Bank, has played. As David Crane notes, "Stiglitz has taken it upon himself to challenge what he calls the 'Washington consensus' — the prevailing orthodoxy of the International Monetary Fund, Organization for Economic Co-operation and Development, Group of Seven industrialized nations' finance ministers and conservative finance ministers."

Referring to this orthodoxy, Stiglitz himself says, "There was never a presumption that markets yielded an optimal societal or generational distribution of income, and now there does not seem to be any basis for the presumption that markets yield efficient outcomes." Moreover, he asserts, history clearly shows that government has played "a significant positive public role in the countries with the most successful development strategies, including the United States and East Asia."

He further believes that those who have been critical of the Asian economic miracle, particularly in the aftermath of the region's financial meltdown, "overlook the successes of the past three decades, to which the government, despite occasional mistakes, has certainly contributed. These achievements, which include not only big increases in per capita domestic product but also increases in life expectancy, the extension of education, and a dramatic reduction of poverty, are real and will prove more lasting than the current financial turmoil."

Impressively, Stiglitz reminds us that we need broader goals than economic growth alone. "We seek increases in living standards — including improved health and education — not just increases in measured GDP. We seek sustainable development, which includes preserving natural resources and maintaining a healthy environment. We seek equitable development, which ensures that all groups in society, not just those at the top, enjoy the fruits of development. And we seek democratic development, in which citizens participate in a variety of ways in making the decisions that affect their lives."

THE THIRD WAY IN HISTORY

In reminding us of the many successes of the Asian economic development model, Stiglitz also demonstrates that the Third Way has very deep historical roots, not only in Canada, as we have argued, but also in Germany, Japan, and East Asia.

Those of us who live in the Anglo-American world have a curiously narrow view of economic theory. In *Looking at the Sun*, a stimulating book on Japan and the Asian economic miracle, American author James Fallows describes how other nations, principally Japan and Germany, have enjoyed tremendous economic development while ignoring what we would regard as standard economic orthodoxy. In one chapter, entitled "The Idea of Economic Success," Fallows makes a startling observation. He argues that many in the Anglo-American world have assumed that the economic principles of Adam Smith, laid out in 1776 in *The Wealth of Nations* and reinforced in the subsequent writings of David Ricardo, Alfred Marshall, and other giants of neo-classical economics, are as universally true and immutable as Newton's laws of physics.

> . . . the assumption behind the Anglo-American model is that if you take care of the individuals, the communities and nations will take care of themselves. Some communities will suffer, as dying industries and inefficient producers go down, but other communities will rise. And as for nations as a whole, they are not assumed to have economic interests — apart from the narrow field of national defense. There is no general "American" or "British" economic interest beyond the welfare of the individual consumers who happen to live inside its borders.

But what would happen, asks Fallows, if it turned out that the Germans, the Japanese, and other successful Asian nations were following some other model, some other primary text, some other basic rules of economics that had nothing to do with Adam Smith? And what would happen if this alternative set of rules worked just fine for them — indeed, worked even better over the last thirty years than our rules, almost as if a completely different understanding of physics was as powerful in explaining the behaviour of matter as Newtonian physics?

It turns out that the Germans and Japanese have been working under a different set of assumptions about the way economics works. Their starting point is an obscure (to us) nineteenth-century German economist, Friedrich List, whose book *The National System of Political Economy* has exercised a powerful influence in the non-Anglo-American world. Fallows explains the basis of his theory in this way:

> The German view was more concerned with the welfare — indeed, sovereignty — of people in groups, in communities, in nations. This is its most obvious link with the Asian economic development strategy of today. Friedrich List fulminated against "cosmopolitan theorists" who assumed away the fact that people lived in nations and that their welfare depended to some degree on how their neighbours fared. If you make $100,000 and everyone around you makes $80,000, you feel well off. The community is prosperous, and you are a success. If you make $101,000 and everyone around you is a destitute beggar, you are worse off in any full reckoning of human well-being, even though your standing is higher in both absolute and relative terms. This, in a nutshell, is the case that today's Japanese make against the American economy: American managers and professionals live more opulently than their counterparts in Japan, but they have to guard themselves physically (and morally) against the down-and-out people with whom they share the country.

List himself wrote in *The National System*: "Between each individual and the entire humanity, however, stands the NATION, with its special language and literature, with its peculiar origin and history, with its special manners and customs, laws and institutions, with the claims of all these for existence, independence, perfection, and continuance for the future, and with its separate territory; a society which, united by a thousand ties of mind and interest, combined itself into one independent whole."

As Fallows makes clear, the profound differences between the Anglo-American view of economics and that of the Germans and Japanese are also indicators of profound differences in societal values. What Americans have found particularly galling about the Asian economic miracle of the past thirty years is that it was viewed as a repudiation not only of the American way of doing business, but also of the American way of life. Little wonder, then, that as Asian economies came crashing down in the latter half of 1997, many American commentators were positively gloating at the apparent affirmation of American political, economic, and social superiority. In an article in the *Wall Street Journal* entitled "Sayonara Japan Inc.," historian Ron Chernow celebrated the collapse of Japan's banking and corporate structure. "The archaic Japanese system has now lost its logic," he wrote. Others, such as Edward Lincoln, a senior fellow at the Brookings Institution in Washington, asserted that Asian countries like South Korea had done badly by following the Japanese economic model and should have followed the American one instead. It was payback time for the American triumphalists.

CANADA AND THE THIRD WAY

In the Third Way, Canadians can find a response to the challenges of globalization that is familiar and unthreatening — indeed, a response we have been formulating through our values and actions for some time. One might argue, without being overtly partisan, that this is a classical Liberal response, or a response with which Red Tories or the old Ontario Conservatives might be comfortable. Significantly, the New Democratic Party, at both the provincial level (in Saskatchewan under Premier Roy Romanow) and more recently the national level (under Alexa McDonough), has also begun to see itself as a party of inclusion, moving along a path like that of Tony Blair's New Labour Party in Britain.

So how can we advance the principles of the Third Way in Canada in a way that is not only morally and rhetorically satisfying, but also sufficiently tough-minded to meet the test of reality? One place to begin is by noting what *doesn't* work: the increasingly high cost to societies that choose the route of confrontation over cooperation. In Canada, the recent political history of Ontario perfectly illustrates the case. It can be reasonably argued that the long-reigning Conservative governments of George Drew, Leslie Frost, John Robarts, and Bill Davis were broad-based, centrist, inclusive, and consensual in style. Benefiting from, but also contributing to, a long run of post-Second World War prosperity, these governments created the social and economic infrastructure that allowed Ontario to flourish in an atmosphere of social peace. Indeed, the success of this strategy was manifested in the extraordinarily long political tenure the Conservatives enjoyed.

During Liberal premier David Peterson's comparatively brief time in office, the essential elements of this broad-based approach were preserved. As with the Conservatives, the Liberal government was not perceived to be defending the interests of one group of Ontarians against another. The Conservatives and the Liberals were not political fundamentalists, nor were they class- or interest-based, but rather both were parties composed of pragmatists who attempted to reach out to all sectors of society for support.

But with the surprise election of the New Democrats under Bob Rae in 1990, the formula for political success in Ontario changed dramatically, not so much because of Bob Rae himself, but because of a combination of worsening economic circumstances and the remarkable short-sightedness of the party's core supporters. To the fury of his own unionized rank and file, Rae imposed the so-called Social Contract and "Rae days" on public sector employees, with the laudable intention of reducing the biggest single item of government expense, salaries, in the most humane way possible.

Rae's admirable attempt to think beyond the narrow interests of his traditional supporters for the common good of all in a time of crisis turned out to be a doubly disastrous strategy. First, the very people who had the most to gain by keeping him in power — trade unionists, teachers, health care workers, environmentalists, social activists — were so determined to punish his "betrayal" that they failed to support him in the next election, thereby ushering in a Conservative government that turned out to be their worst nightmare. Second, these so-called supporters were so vociferous in their demands that they created the false impression that the government, rather than acting in the interests of the entire province, had been taken over by a bunch of left-wing loonies.

Thus began in Ontario the era of what might rudely be described as "silly bugger" politics. This is the politics of organized class warfare, in which the political game is seen as one of "ins" and "outs." We throw out the bleeding hearts, the tree-huggers, the trade unions, the social workers, and the gays, and then we vote in the folks from the "905" belt of suburban Torontonians, with their allies in the business community, small towns, and rural areas. In a remarkable break with tradition, the triumphant Tories did not even attempt to broaden their base of support, did not even try to govern for all Ontarians, but focused instead on a strategy of "narrowcasting" to the 43 percent of voters who are their core supporters, confident that if the Liberals and NDP continued to split the majority vote, they could come marching right down the middle. The Tories analyzed Bob Rae's brave attempt to govern on behalf of all of Ontario's citizens and drew their own cynical conclusions.

It is certainly possible to argue that many of the reforms introduced by the provincial Tories were overdue and necessary. It is not, however, possible to argue that the way in which the reforms were introduced, whether in the area of health care, education, the environment, or the mega-merger of Toronto, preserved both the best elements of the institutions targeted and the climate of constructive social peace so necessary for navigating difficult periods of economic change. In so carelessly destroying carefully nurtured institutions and social capital in the name of brainless free market ideology, the Tories have, ironically enough, perhaps made it more difficult for Ontario to emerge as either a more efficient economic entity or a better society in terms of human development. Class conflict has its costs.

The recent experience of Ontario under the Conservatives (and, one might add, British Columbia under the NDP) is a working, homegrown example of the Canada we most emphatically don't want, a Canada in which goofy, misunderstood concepts of globalization have produced either a slavish adherence to the principles of the market or a Pavlovian overreaction against them.

To promote the concept of the Third Way in Canada is to argue that when celebrated economist Joseph Schumpeter exuberantly preached the value of the "creative destruction" of capitalism, he did not at the same time envisage the creative (or otherwise) destruction of the free societies that nurture capitalism in the first place. *Pace* Ian Angell, economies do not exist in a void completely detached from human society.

Canada's finance minister Paul Martin spoke to the 1998 Couchiching Conference on the subject of rethinking Canada for the twenty-first century.

At the heart of globalization lies an inherent bias towards inequality. The immediate availability of virtually unlimited choice means that we are creating a world where the best will do very well but where second best will fall far, far behind. This cannot help but exacerbate the existing disparity between a small number of winners and everyone else. . . .

The great nations of the twenty-first century will be those who recognize the incomparable value of a vibrant and expanding middle class. One where the gap between rich and poor is constantly narrowed. Where the mainstream is constantly widened. Where the quality of life is lifted for all so that even the most vulnerable among us can be assured of a better future. . . .

No one can take on the challenges of the new economy while preoccupied with the availability of basic care. No parent of an ill child. And no child of an ageing parent. Medicare. Employment Insurance. Public pensions. Individually these each address a critical need. Collectively, they form a foundation of personal security — a platform for greater achievement.

TOWARDS A CIVIL SOCIETY

In our view of what the Third Way means for Canada, the first two ways are the way of government and the way of the market. But the Third Way is not simply splitting the difference between these or balancing two sets of competing interests; it is formally recognizing and injecting into the debate the concept of a third element, which has often been defined as "civil society."

In his run for the leadership of the federal Progressive Conservatives, Hugh Segal defined civil society as that "part of life that is beyond the reach of the government and beyond the reach of the marketplace. . . . It reflects our genuine desire to find meaning in the lives we live with others, in the communities we share and in the help our presence and support provides for those around us."

It should be noted here that the term "civil society" has come to have three meanings. First, it refers to the third sector, the part of society that is not business or government, and includes voluntary associations, churches, clubs, and charities. The second meaning is broader and is sometimes identified as "civic society" or "civic community"; this involves all the elements of society, including business, government, and the voluntary sector, coming together for the collective promotion of citizenship and social and economic well-being. The third meaning is the more traditional and commonsensical one: a society characterized by the civility of its inhabitants. All three have relevance for this discussion (although you will find that not everyone who uses the term clarifies which of these meanings is uppermost in his or her mind).

The whole concept of civil society has been enjoying something of a resurgence of late. Countries in both the developing world and the former Soviet empire are being actively encouraged by the West to strengthen mechanisms of good governance and civil society. Indeed, civil society is seen as an integral part of good governance, an indispensable component of both mature and emerging democracies.

The guru of the civil society movement is American political scientist

Robert Putnam, author of one of the most influential books of the decade, *Making Democracy Work*, published in 1993. For those who have not read the book, the subtitle — *Civic Traditions in Modern Italy* — might, at first glance, seem a little surprising. But in the words of the publisher, "Putnam and his collaborators offer empirical evidence for the importance of 'civic community' in developing successful institutions. Their focus is on a unique experiment begun in 1970 when Italy created new governments for each of its regions. After spending two decades analyzing the efficacy of these governments in such fields as agriculture, housing, and health services, they reveal patterns of associationism, trust, and cooperation that facilitate good governance and economic prosperity."

A crucial part of Putnam's argument is that the enormous differences between the various parts of Italy are wholly attributable to history and geography. Another central element to his thesis is the importance of "social capital." In his words, "Social capital typically consists in ties, norms, and trust transferable from one social setting to another. Members of Florentine choral societies participate because they like to sing, not because their participation strengthens the Tuscan social fabric. But it does."

It might be argued that of the three elements that comprise Canadian society — government, business, and civil society — civil society is the magic part; the part that humanizes and informs the first two; the part that over time actually allows the first two to work; the part that is the fundamental purpose and goal of the first two; the part that adds value and makes life in society worth living; the part that *is* value, decency, civility, and civilization itself.

Yet for all of our new awareness of the importance of civil society in Canada, it is a concept that is also under attack in various parts of the country. In Quebec, newspaper columnist Lysiane Gagnon has drawn attention to the work of sociologist Gary Caldwell. Caldwell wrote an essay, entitled "The Decay of Civil Society in Contemporary Quebec," analyzing the cause of "our languishing public culture," which he attributes, in part, to confusion over social ethics. "When individuals do not know what to do in public situations, they effectively do nothing," wrote Caldwell. "This means not assuming a post in a voluntary association, not acting to prevent conflicts of interest or not coming to the aid of a fellow citizen in distress. The failure of more than a hundred young men to react during the Polytechnique massacre of 1989 is revealing in this respect."

Caldwell attributes this phenomenon, in part, to "the vertiginous destabilization of the family as an institution" (Quebec is the province with the greatest proportion of unmarried parents and the highest divorce rate in Canada). Another cause of a weakened civil society, claims Caldwell, is an overdeveloped state technocracy. Lysiane Gagnon offers the following summary of Caldwell's argument: "In the 1960s' Quiet Revolution, the state replaced the Roman Catholic Church; this was progress, but some of the results are problematic. The population went directly from the tutelage of one institution to that of another without having the opportunity to develop a set of non-religious values, a code of civic ethics and a sense of personal responsibility for the well-being of fellow citizens."

But Quebec is not alone in this regard. Ironically, another province in which civil society is jeopardized is Ontario. We say "ironically" because the Conservative government of Mike Harris has dedicated itself to reducing, not increasing, the power of the state and relying on volunteer organizations to fill the gap. It turns out, however, that too little government can be as bad for civil society as too much, because too little government places too great a burden on the voluntary and community-based parts of society. As Dalton Camp has noted, "It needs to be said that much of the infrastructure of the voluntary associations in the civil society are underwritten or given subsidy by governments and could not survive without them and remain effective."

The acknowledged strategy of the Harris team has been to rely on volunteers to make up for those services abandoned by the government.

The Ontario Tories' Common Sense Revolution literature explains this by way of an example: "Studies have found that children who go to school hungry do poorly in class, are more disruptive and suffer more health problems. With leadership from our Premier, and with private sector and volunteer support, a breakfast nutrition program can be implemented at little or no cost to taxpayers." But how do volunteers make sure all children are covered? How do volunteers deal with the underlying causes of poverty and disrupted family life, which explain why the children arrive at school hungry in the first place?

It turns out in the end that the Harris Tories don't really believe that more vibrant civic and voluntary associations are the answer after all, because these smack of collectivism. The moment the word "group" is invoked, the qualifiers "special" and "interest" are quickly added. One has only to think of the short shrift and disrespect accorded hospital boards, school boards, environmental organizations, and municipal bodies to realize how little faith the Harris government really has in the institutions of civil society. As political scientist Rob Vipond has observed:

> The Tories are so relentlessly individualistic that it is almost impossible for them to believe that any social group (with the possible exception of political parties) can be anything but a necessary evil. This is one reason the government has gone out of its way in its first term to marginalize the role of social associations in the policy process — including many of the voluntary associations that are now providing services that the government once provided. And that is why the government is so enthusiastic about having all tax increases submitted to referendums. If groups invariably distort and obstruct the policy process, referendums provide a way for governments to go over their heads to individual voters. Yet all of this, to repeat, produces a dilemma: the Tories can't live with civic associations, and they can't live without them.

A CIVIL SOCIETY STRATEGY FOR CANADA

If the Third Way depends on a thriving civil society to function — if civil society does, indeed, provide the magic — then it is time we thought long and hard about the future of civil society in Canada.

Some of the clearest and most visionary thinking on this subject can be found in the work of Sherri Torjman of the Ottawa-based Caledon Institute, a public policy think-tank. In a 1997 paper entitled "Civil Society: Reclaiming our Humanity," she lays out very eloquently not only the fundamental principles of civil society, but also strategies for implementing those principles. Her vision is clear:

> A civil society sustains and enhances the capacity of all of its members to build a caring and mutually responsible society. It means that all citizens — individual, corporate, and government — assume responsibility for promoting economic, social, and environmental well-being.
>
> A civil society seeks to achieve three main objectives. It builds and strengthens caring communities. It ensures economic security. It promotes social investment by directing resources towards the well-being and positive development of people.

According to Torjman, the crucial difference between the way we have traditionally thought about these laudable goals and a civil society approach lies in the *means* by which such objectives are to be achieved. "First, a civil society interprets very broadly the concept of resources to include — but move well beyond — the notion of public dollars. Second, a civil society encourages the creation of partnerships and collaborative working arrangements to achieve its objectives. Finally, a civil society understands the connection between the dots; it addresses issues in a holistic and integrated way." (As the next chapter will show, this succinct description of civil society might well also serve as a description of what we call National Projects.)

In outlining a conceptual framework for a civil society strategy, Torjman draws on contemporary thinking about sustainable development. The approach to sustainable development is holistic, integrating economic, social, and environmental concerns; at the centre of civil society is human well-being, which cannot flourish in the absence of both a healthy environment and a buoyant economy. Sustainable development also stresses the importance of intergenerational bonds; we know we cannot meet today's needs at the expense of future generations.

Another characteristic that is important to both sustainable development and civil society is the approach to problem-solving. "The concept is framed on the notion that solutions to complex problems are best addressed through multisectoral dialogue and collaborative approaches," explains Torjman. "All sectors, including governments, business, labour, education, foundations and social agencies, must take responsibility for tackling economic, social and environmental issues." One of the chief goals of civil society, of course, is to build caring communities, which implies, in turn, that we pay particular attention to the concept of citizenship in all its forms: individual, corporate, organizational, and governmental. Citizenship also carries with it the twin ideas of rights and responsibilities.

Torjman cites the work of the American Civic Forum in promoting the need for citizens to become change agents and public problem-solvers in communities. The forum argues that one way to build caring communities is through a healthy third sector, "that vibrant array of voluntary organizations, religious congregations, schools and colleges, the free press, professional groups, and community organizations that mediate between government and the market." These institutions of civil society, these places where people come together in communities, can provide both the leadership and the sites for public problem-solving, skill-building, and experimentation. These institutions are the "social capital" to which Robert Putnam referred, the civic virtue that expresses and builds trust and cooperation among all citizens in a society.

The American Civic Forum notes that a rich public life rests on three key features: a commitment to build the capacities of individuals and communities; an emphasis on deliberative public dialogue and debate; and a focus on practical problem-solving that, without requiring consensus on values, allows diverse players to collaborate on getting things done.

But as Torjman notes, "The danger in promoting more active citizenship is that it inadvertently can encourage governments to abrogate their responsibility for economic, social and environmental well-being. Yet the opposite is actually required. Governments have a central role to play in supporting citizen involvement in public and community problem-solving. Moreover, government's role with respect to income redistribution and social investment is more important than ever." Mike Harris take note.

If building caring communities is the first essential element of civil society, the second and third are economic security and social investment. But for all three, an important feature is leverage. Torjman gives many examples of ways in which financial and human capital can be leveraged, including, for instance, better mobilizing the energies of youth and seniors.

Leverage, in turn, requires partnerships and collaboration. "Partnerships are important for several reasons," she notes. "They help raise awareness of pressing social problems, such as poverty and family violence, and broaden the range of sectors taking responsibility for economic, social, and environmental well-being. These arrangements harness previously untapped resources in new and creative ways, thereby increasing the amount of total investment in a given concern." But there is one paramount reason for acting together. "Partnerships and collaboratives also embody a clear and important message: Economic, social, and environmental issues are the concern of the entire community — not simply of governments or social agencies. Moreover, all sectors are responsible for addressing these problems — preferably through a planned and coordinated approach that combines resources and expertise in new and sustainable ways."

None of this, however, can be a substitute for the role of government. "Partnerships and collaboratives both complement and supplement the public sector," explains Torjman. "They can never and should never be expected to replace the role of government in redistributing income, making essential social investments and building caring communities through the promotion of citizenship."

Finally, one of the greatest strengths of civil society should be its ability to take a holistic approach, seeing the interrelationships among and between various aspects of human well-being. Notes Torjman:

> The satisfaction of economic needs requires a strong social base which promotes social well-being; the satisfaction of social needs, in turn, requires a solid economic base.
>
> Social well-being also depends to a large extent on good health, which is influenced by both education and income security. Educational attainment is affected by many factors, including health, self-esteem and income. . . . Civil society sees these issues as a set of interrelated factors rather than as discrete categories — the approach typically employed by governments to deal with problems.

A civil society approach is an efficient strategy in human terms for Canada. Rather than dealing with human problems by putting them in jail, walling them off from gated communities, writing them off as social failures, or abandoning them as Ian Angell would advise, a civil society finds ways of mobilizing people through training, education, and most important, participation. In so doing, they convert citizens who were previously thought of as liabilities into assets.

More broadly, whether we speak of the Third Way or the full involvement of civil society, we know that if Canadians act together, this is the strategy best suited to the complexity of many of our contemporary challenges. We know that we cannot solve complex environmental problems, such as the reduction of greenhouse gases, by acting as individuals. We know that if we are ever to create a truly national system of innovation, this will require the mobilization of all our resources. We know that a relatively small country like Canada cannot hope to compete globally if our key industries are not supported as part of a national system.

In advancing this vision of Canada, we recognize that we are proposing competing as a team against our international rivals. Such a team-based society understands the foolishness of competition between governments, or between business and labour, or between business and environmentalists. Such a society sets national goals and then asks how all of us, working together, can achieve them.

A society of reciprocal obligation is a society that can try new things and take risks — because those risks are shared by all of us. A society of reciprocal obligation encourages its citizens to experiment and to innovate, recognizing that only through trial and error can individuals, companies, governments, and societies ever improve.

If we focus on our assets and opportunities, if we work to find creative solutions to old and new problems, if we approach our task with a sense of hope and shared adventure, we will restore Canadians' faith in themselves and their government. A country that solves its own problems, that competes successfully with others, becomes not only more powerful and independent, but also a model and inspiration for other nations around the world.

5

National Projects

Occasionally, we have glimpses of how Canada ought to be, of the Canada We Want. For the older generation, this might come from the memory of a country united and full of purpose during the Second World War. For others, it might be seen in the extraordinary response of Canadians to the African famine crisis of 1984. More recently, we saw glimpses in the outpouring of support from across the country during the floods in the Saguenay and in Manitoba, and during the ice storm in southern Quebec and eastern Ontario. Perhaps some of us see it in the annual Team Canada trade mission, with the prime minister, the provincial premiers, and various business people working together on behalf of the whole country to sell Canadian goods and services in some distant part of the world. Perhaps the glimpse may come every two years, as we lay aside our regional differences and cheer for our summer and winter Olympic teams.

But why do we understand the Team Canada approach so clearly when it comes to sports and foreign trade and so vaguely when it comes to dealing with domestic affairs? Why does it take a national or international crisis to draw us together as a nation, and why do we revert to our foolish, divisive ways once the crisis is over? What strange country is this where we are mostly cautious and prudent, and only occasionally bold, risk-taking, innovative, and adventurous? Why don't we realize that the Canada We Want lives as much in our hearts as in our heads?

There is a political theory that contrasts official politics with the "politics of desire." The politics of desire is the politics of longing, the deep unconscious fears and hopes of people, which rarely find expression in official politics. The politics of desire can be found in the innermost feelings of a people oppressed by a dictatorship. It can also be found when a charismatic leader discovers, within his own personality, beliefs and desires that resonate with an entire population. The so-called Bouchard effect is an example of this from our own society.

In our collective struggle to preserve the unity of Canada, the politics of desire has the potential to be a decisive force for either good or ill. In the hands of a Lucien Bouchard, who speaks of "us" and "them," of "the Quebec people," of "a real country," it is the politics of inclusion and exclusion, of the conflicting passions of fear and hope. And the negative side can also be seen in the politics of regional resentment as practised by provincial premiers who routinely campaign against the federal government. It was this type of politics of desire that caused B.C.'s Glen Clark, when confronted with the catastrophic disappearance of West Coast salmon, to accuse the federal fisheries minister, David Anderson, of treason.

This raising of the emotional stakes is typical of the politics of desire, and it is a dangerous game because it can lead to irrational, uncontrollable actions. Author Terry Glavin describes the mood of helpless despair that grips B.C. fishing communities as a kind of "medieval delirium." "Hopeless fish-war stratagems, which the Pacific Salmon Treaty has failed to contain, are played out as though salmon runs were just enemy flags fluttering over a battlefield," he notes. "Fishing-industry warlords dispatch boats against one another like catapults and siege wagons." This is the ideal breeding ground for regional resentment.

Another negative form of the politics of desire is the politics of social resentment. In Ontario, Mike Harris's Conservatives were elected on the basis of promises that seemed reasonable but hid a deeper, coded meaning. For instance, Harris promised to introduce work-fare in the name of giving people on welfare the dignity of a job. (Translation: We're going to make sure those shiftless, lazy welfare bums work for their money.) In the name of fairness, Harris said he would end equity legislation that discriminated against average non-minority people. (Translation: There are too many damn immigrants here anyway, and it's time nice white, middle-class folks like us got their jobs back.)

Faced with these and other negative examples of the politics of desire, how do we create a larger, more generous vision of Canada that is both rational and sensible while still appealing to our nobler emotions, dreams, and love of country? How do we awaken the deeper feelings and hopes of Canadians to forge a pan-Canadian politics of desire? And do Canadians wish to be awakened? Do we want to be bold and adventurous? Are we in any mood for this kind of thinking and feeling?

The 1980s and 1990s have been testing times for Canada. Governments overspent. Businesses shed jobs. Canadians found their living standards declining. Economic growth sputtered. Faced with the threat of financial collapse, federal and provincial governments in the 1990s made their first order of business the restoration of public finances. But slashing budgets necessitated painful program cuts. With key programs like health, education, and social assistance facing reductions to their core funding, neither governments nor citizens were in any mood or position to contemplate new spending. Indeed, all governments were faced with a pervasive scepticism about their ability to do anything in the face of the huge challenges brought about by technological change and global competition. There was a feeling of helpless resignation as Canadians contemplated their future.

Now, in the late 1990s, the situation and the mood have changed. Governments have not only brought their finances under control, they have also, in some cases, registered surpluses. Employment rates have improved. Economic growth has strengthened. So what do we do now?

Certainly, many of us are still not happy with the current state of affairs. Despite its decline, the unemployment rate remains a persistent problem. And nobody likes to see provincial governments continuing to bicker with the federal government and with each other. Few also believe that the threat of Quebec separatism has gone away. On the whole, there remains a sense of division in the land — division between regions, division between classes. For many people, particularly young Canadians, the future still seems dark. Increasing numbers feel excluded from the economy, from political life, from society itself.

But beneath the gloom, Canadians are recovering their fundamental sense of optimism. The challenge for our society is to find concrete ways for its citizens to channel and express this optimism. Polling data reveal that there is a widely shared desire for harmony in Canada, a desire for social reconciliation rather than class warfare, a desire to see governments working together rather than squabbling over power.

Above all, there is a desire for inclusion — for full participation in the economy as members of the workforce, for full participation socially as contributors to the community, and for full participation politically as citizens. Canadians do not wish their governments to treat them simply as consumers and clients; they want to be treated as citizens. And citizens have more than an economic stake in the country; they have a social, political, cultural, and moral stake as well.

Most Canadians would concede that over the past few years, their governments have done a better job of getting their fiscal houses in order, of building a firmer financial foundation. But a foundation for what? Our challenge is to find a vision of a Canada fit for the twenty-first century to which all Canadians can subscribe. But for a vision to become a reality, we need to set for ourselves achievable and measurable goals. We need to imagine and realize the great National Projects that will allow us to attain these goals. We need to set out timelines and priorities. We need to be able to measure progress and results. Most of all, we need to involve all Canadians in the execution of these National Projects, because it is only with all of us acting together that we can recover our optimism and hope as a country.

National Projects. What do we mean by this term? Here is one of the best definitions, put forward by writer David Olive in February 1996:

Certainly we all want national unity. But what is our national purpose? What is our national project, the thing that binds our 30 million souls to a single, uplifting idea? Surely it isn't the quest to get by with 20% fewer hospital beds, or the effort to boost productivity ratios, or clever ways to cut spending on social programs. That is an accountant's dream of national unity, and it shouldn't be any surprise that it appeals only to other accountants.

In earlier times, our unifying project was to build the basic infrastructure of a nation: roads, railways, a national broadcasting service. Later, our national project was to reinforce this foundation with a social infrastructure of old age pensions, unemployment insurance, subsidized university tuition, welfare assistance and quality health care available to all, regardless of income or social standing. Our past politicians and political leaders, for all their shortcomings, did not fail us in these projects. We can look to their work for the explanation of why the United Nations persists in finding that the sun shines more brightly over this part of the planet than others.

But in recent years, what has been the mission that rallies us to a cause we call Canada, what values and vision make ours a country that Canadians in Quebec and elsewhere can respond to with a sense of affirmation and affection?

Proving that he had more than the soul of an accountant, Paul Martin, Canada's finance minister, used similar language in his February 1996 budget speech.

Successful countries do more than occupy a place on a map. They live in the souls of their people because they are relevant to the betterment of their lives.

And so for Canada it is time to set the goals anchored in our shared values and our shared aspirations. We have done that throughout our history, in the days when we dared speak of a national dream and then built it; in the days when we aspired to a kinder society and then created it. . . .

We must set great national challenges, not small ones, because it is only by reaching as high as we are able that we will discover how far we can go.

So what are National Projects? At their most basic, they are simply projects that have all of us united for a common purpose. And they are not *federal* projects, they are *national*. They require all levels of government — federal, provincial, and municipal — to work together. They require the participation of the public and private sectors, of trade unions and social activists, of professionals and volunteers, of all citizens.

The role of the federal government in promoting National Projects is to think of the common interests of all Canadians. The federal government has to call the meeting. The federal government must put before Canadians a series of goals and invite their comments and participation. The federal government must act as a strategic broker in forming the partnerships that can achieve the National Projects, for they are of such a scope and scale that no sector of society can achieve them in isolation. National Projects allow us to mobilize all our resources as a country to achieve a great collective purpose. National Projects remind us why we need a country in the first place.

Recently, the idea behind such National Projects has been expressed in a variety of ways. The term "millennium projects" might have been an acceptable alternative, but for its overuse and consequent trivialization (what isn't a millennium project these days?). The Canadian Policy Research Network, referring to large-scale social programs, speaks of Canadian projects. In Quebec, the term *projet de société* conveys the exact sense of a National Project. It is a societal project, because it requires a partnership of all parts of society.

NATIONAL PROJECTS BEFORE 1945

The basic idea of the National Project is as old as the country itself. As we have seen, Canadians have always been far readier to act collectively than Americans, partly because geography and history have forced us to do so. The ultimate National Project (apart from Confederation in 1867, of course) was John A. Macdonald's National Policy in the 1870s, a conscious attempt to work against the natural gravitational pull of the United States by building an economic system that worked from east to west.

The building of the railway across Canada in the 1870s and 1880s — the National Dream — was not only the stuff of legend, but also a physical expression of the politics of desire. This National Project could not have been completed without the focus and dedication of the entire national community. The unprecedented partnership of the federal government with private enterprise and the necessary cooperation with the provinces, territories, and municipalities are the hallmarks of a great National Project. The opening of the Canadian West in the 1890s and early 1900s required an equal national effort.

Canada's participation in the First World War eventually required a total economic and social mobilization to achieve a common purpose. No citizen was immune to this National Project. In the name of winning the war, all interests were subordinated to the greater good. The federal government, the provinces, all industry, all workers, all farms, all mines, all citizens, willingly or not, worked together to defeat Germany.

The creation of the CBC in the 1930s came about as a conscious decision by the government of Canada to counteract the influence of American culture through the new medium of radio. The government decided to regulate broadcasting and create a national, publicly owned radio service modelled on the British Broadcasting Corporation. No other entity could have done it.

But for Canadians, the greatest National Project of the first half of the twentieth century was undoubtedly the Second World War. The mission statement was clear: defeat Hitler and the Axis powers whatever the cost. Nothing less than the total engagement of Canadian society and the economy would do. Nothing, not even Maurice Duplessis's recalcitrant nationalist, pacifist government in Quebec, would be allowed to get in the way. This was Canada Inc. at war, long before the phenomenon called Quebec Inc. came along in the 1960s.

HOW TO RECOGNIZE A NATIONAL PROJECT

If we stand back from this historical excursion and try to discern the broad characteristics that many of these National Projects, and those described in Chapter 3, shared, it is possible to identify a dozen main elements.

1. All of the National Projects of the past were undertaken because there was a perceived need to resolve some urgent problem, and there was some element of agreement, at least among the country's leaders, about the nature of the solution.
2. Only a very few National Projects could be undertaken at one time because of the huge demand they placed on society's resources, and because of the need for governments to focus their leadership, administrative, and fiscal capacities.
3. The federal government facilitated these projects because they could not have been initiated by provincial or municipal governments or the

private sector alone. National Projects frequently involved a partnership with the private sector. The building of the Canadian Pacific Railway and the Trans-Canada Pipeline were both the result of partnerships between the federal government and private enterprise, and both needed the cooperation of the provinces. Thus these projects were societal, inclusive, collectivist enterprises, which is why they should be called National Projects, not Federal Projects.

4. Each National Project had a clearly stated mission, which allowed citizens to measure outcomes and judge whether the project had been a success or a failure. The mission of Macdonald's National System in the 1870s was to reorient the Canadian economy from north-south to east-west. The mission of building the railway was to link Canada from coast to coast. The mission of public health insurance was to ensure equitable access to the health care system for all.

5. Each National Project built on existing assets and potential competitive advantages, which, in turn, mobilized broad support across Canada in all sectors. When, for example, the federal government decided in the 1950s to support the arts more actively, it was able to supplement an existing base of music, dance, theatre, and training facilities. The same was true of public health insurance in the 1950s and 1960s.

6. Every National Project proceeded with a clearly understood and declared belief in how things worked and hence why the project was being undertaken. If you built a railway, you would not only defend your sovereignty against the Americans (and, incidentally, any pesky internal dissidents), you would also attract immigrants to the West and allow goods to flow more efficiently. Every National Project was based on a theory, be that theory economic, social, or cultural.

7. National Projects often embodied a paradigm shift, which, in turn, reinforced systemic changes in some major societal system, such as transportation, health, social welfare, defence, or culture. The birth of the Canadian Broadcasting Corporation in the 1930s represented a

radical shift in the way Canadians thought about the emerging technology of radio, which ceased to be a local enterprise and became a national service capable of connecting Canadians wherever they happened to live. The advent of public health insurance radically altered perceptions about how medicine and the health care system worked, because it removed the element of random access that had been the reality for most lower-income Canadians.

8. National Projects were undertaken with passion, a sense of mission, a sense of vision. There was excitement and a feeling of purpose and resolve in the air. Not surprisingly, these projects were also highly controversial and evoked emotional debates, precisely because they so often represented a new way of doing things. But because there was an element of challenge and adversity, National Projects often engendered a sense of common enterprise and shared adventure, a sense of living in a real country, a country that pulls together.

9. It is axiomatic that National Projects demanded leadership and risk-taking. Sometimes that leadership was provincial, as was the case when Tommy Douglas's CCF government in Saskatchewan introduced public health insurance and challenged the rest of the country to do likewise. But often, it was federal, precisely because the federal government has a legitimate responsibility to look out for national interests and see how creative provincial initiatives might be generalized across the country.

10. Both the undertaking and the achievement of these National Projects were a source of national pride, with the marked collateral benefit of strengthening national unity. National Projects gave us the feeling of national solidarity.

11. Once achieved, our National Projects became embedded in the value structure — indeed, in the mythology — of the nation. We now think of ourselves as distinct from other people, particularly Americans, because we built the CPR, we created the CBC, we developed public health insurance. Such things define us as Canadians, as a nation

unique on the planet. Politicians tamper with such icons at their peril.

12. Finally, our National Projects reminded us why we had a country in the first place: to achieve things together as a society, as a national community, that we could not achieve alone or in our constituent parts. Our National Projects were the essence of nationhood itself.

SO WHATEVER HAPPENED TO NATIONAL PROJECTS?

Despite the economic turmoil of the 1970s, 1980s, and 1990s, National Projects did not entirely disappear outside Quebec. Rather, they became less frequent and more modest in scale and scope, and evolved into what we call Strategic Opportunities.

Strategic Opportunities have many of the same characteristics as National Projects, but not all of them. A good example of a successful Strategic Opportunity — Canada's commitment to Arctic surveillance beginning in the 1970s — was described by former Arctic scientist James Rossiter at a conference on National Projects organized by John Godfrey in Toronto in March 1996. According to Dr. Rossiter, there were two events which triggered a recognition that Canada needed to improve its Arctic surveillance. One was the 1969 voyage of the American icebreaker *Manhattan* through Canadian Arctic waters, which was seen as a clear threat to Canadian sovereignty. The second was the oil crisis of 1973, which led us to recognize that oil and gas development in the Arctic was a potentially important component of economic self-sufficiency.

Having recognized both the threat and the opportunity, Canada supported the development of several key technologies, such as airborne and satellite radars, ice-thickness sensors, and advanced marine and land radars, through research and development at federal, university, industrial, and provincial laboratories. Collaboration between government and industry was a crucial component of this Strategic Opportunity.

How did we do it? We encouraged activities at the regional level, thus effectively mobilizing existing resources and expertise across the country.

We coordinated these resources through a highly informal network of information-sharing and field trials, through peer review, and through long-term government support. This support led, in turn, to career commitments by able young people.

What were the outcomes? Several complementary technologies were developed and Canada became the undisputed world leader in the field of Arctic surveillance. This led to these technologies being commercialized globally, even though the problems that had given rise to the Strategic Opportunity had by then disappeared. All of these efforts culminated in the establishment of several world-renowned centres of excellence. The launch of RADARSAT (Canada's first earth-observation satellite) in November 1995 was the initiative of one such centre. A final additional benefit was the enormous sense of national pride that emerged from the whole enterprise.

The Strategic Opportunities approach can be applied to any technology or economic sector, or anywhere else there is potential for collaboration between the public and private sectors, throughout the various regions of the country. Bombardier in aerospace, Nortel in digital switching, CAE Electronics in computer simulation all come to mind. The fundamental difference between Strategic Opportunities and National Projects is that the latter are about systemic change, rather than enabling technologies. As Chapters 8 and 9 will show, the projects involving hydrogen fuel cells and new media would have been classified as Strategic Opportunities had we viewed them simply as technologies that could generate global market share. The reason they are National Projects is because the technologies involved have the potential to transform major societal systems.

Of course, we've had other activities in the 1990s that have had some of the characteristics of National Projects. As mentioned, these include Prime Minister Chrétien's Team Canada trade missions, the national response to the floods in Manitoba and the Saguenay, and the assistance offered victims of the ice storm in southern Ontario and eastern Quebec. And there has also been the enormous effort by governments to reduce their deficits.

The sense of urgency; the all-encompassing scope of the attack; the total commitment and focus of all parts of government; the moral fervour of the enterprise; the setting of clear, measurable goals, and the feeling of accomplishment that came from meeting them — all these are characteristics of a National Project. For Canada, deficit-cutting was a necessary activity in the 1990s, but it alone won't be enough to keep us at the top of the U.N.'s rankings in health, education, and per capita income.

A TIME FOR NATIONAL PROJECTS AGAIN?

Is this the moment for Canadians to begin thinking of National Projects again? One favourable factor is that the federal government and several of the provinces have now moved into a post-deficit era. There are potential financial resources, albeit modest, available.

Another positive element is that, at least at the rhetorical level, there is more talk of federal-provincial cooperation. There are official discussions about strengthening the economic and social union. One concrete sign of improved relations was the successful negotiations leading to the creation of the National Child Benefit System. The question is whether these tentative beginnings can be built upon further.

Another hopeful sign, at least at the federal level, is the new way of doing budgets, which began in February 1998 with the first post-deficit-era budget. Apart from some debt and tax reduction, new spending was focused on a major theme of social and economic reinvestment: supporting post-secondary education. This was done in two ways. First, access for students was improved not only by the creation of a centrepiece Millennium Scholarship Fund, but also by a whole host of related measures: helping students with past and future debt, allowing families to invest more easily in registered education funds, and giving mature students a tax break with child care. At the same time, the research function of universities was strengthened by increasing grants to the major federal research granting institutions, such as the Medical Research Council.

If this pattern were to continue federally and then spread to the provinces, it might be easier to pick an annual National Project of social, economic, or cultural significance on which all governments could focus their efforts. Certainly, Canada has a lot of social, technological, environmental, economic, and cultural challenges worthy of a future National Project. Such projects must be seen, however, not only as occasions for solving problems and easing needs, but also as great, positive opportunities for the country. In the face of continuing challenges to national unity, there is a need, now more than ever before, for the vision, passion, and nation-building that come with National Projects.

OBJECTIONS TO NATIONAL PROJECTS

There are, of course, those who raise serious and substantial objections to National Projects. They fear that embarking on new National Projects would simply lead to a spending binge, plunging us back into a deficit position. This is a reasonable point that can be countered only by our being extremely disciplined, selective, and strategic in our choice of National Projects. The federal government may have found the formula for this in its new budget process, which isolates a main area for social or economic reinvestment.

Overburdened taxpayers, meanwhile, may feel that tax reduction should still be the top priority, and their complaints cannot be ignored. Others would urge governments to make debt reduction the first order of business before there is any new spending.

Provincial governments have been adamant that the federal government not use its spending power to initiate any new social programs without their consent, particularly since the federal government appears to have achieved a surplus financial position before many of the provinces. The problem with this is that by insisting that a majority of the provinces give their approval before any new national social program can be started, the provinces may have set the bar too high. Had that been the criterion for the introduction of public health insurance in the 1960s, for example, we would never have had a national public health care system. There needs to be room for the federal government to respond to experiments and initiatives that may be taken up by only a minority of the provinces at first.

The provinces also argue that their top priority is to restore core funding to existing programs through the Canadian Health and Social Transfer (CHST), which helps fund health care, social assistance, and post-secondary education. Here, the problem is twofold. First, there is no limit to the amount of money that can arguably be put into existing programs. Second, if existing programs always take priority over new ones, it will never be possible to break out of an old way of doing things, even when it can be conclusively demonstrated that the old programs are not meeting, and can never meet, their stated objectives.

This is what happened with The Atlantic Groundfish Strategy (TAGS), which was designed to provide temporary transitional economic support to cod fishermen in Newfoundland and to encourage them to undertake training in order to find new kinds of work. Despite the abject failure of TAGS to meet its second objective, the political pressure to extend the existing program was tremendous, primarily because people couldn't accept the reality that the cod fishery will never be the same again.

The case the provinces make against unilateral federal intrusion in areas of provincial jurisdiction merits serious consideration. But it is crucial that the federal government, in partnership with one or two provinces, be able to test new social, technological, environmental, or economic theories that, if successful, would have relevance for the whole country.

The challenge for the federal government and the provinces is to find new ways of working together, ways that are less recrimination-based, less driven by some misguided Cartesianism that insists on rigid separations of functions based on a constitution drawn up in the mid-nineteenth century.

Those who insist that the solution to our national problems can be found in "ending duplication" and clearly assigning roles between the two levels of government simply fail to take into account the nature of the challenges that confront us as we enter the new millennium. Our nineteenth-century model of government was based on the assumption that all problems could be neatly assigned to either the federal or the provincial governments, and then tidily allocated to one specific department or ministry.

But what happens when the cod fishery in Newfoundland collapses? The Department of Fisheries and Oceans cannot deal with the ensuing human tragedy alone. The problem clearly has both economic and human resource implications. And should there not be a role for the Department of the Environment? And where will we find the objective science required to adjudicate competing claims about fish stocks? Clearly not with the hopelessly compromised scientists of the Department of Fisheries and Oceans. Also, who will negotiate on Canada's behalf with foreign governments and foreign fleets? How many provincial departments of economic development, social welfare, and community affairs need to be involved? And what of the affected municipalities? For that matter, what is the role of private fishing companies and the fishermen's union?

Here, perhaps, is the most compelling reason of all for Canadians to undertake National Projects: they allow us to tackle the large, messy problems of our time as a society. In future chapters, we will be looking in detail at some of these challenges, including the need to improve the life prospects of all young children, the problems and potential opportunities posed by greenhouse gases and global warming, and so on.

We believe there is a lot of room for creativity in how we go about this. We should learn from past National Projects, but not be boxed in by that history. We believe, for example, that some National Projects should be led by specific provinces. Remember: the role of the federal government is to facilitate, which doesn't always mean that it has to lead.

CAN POLITICIANS DO THE JOB?

Perhaps the greatest barrier confronting politicians is the deep cynicism of our fellow citizens. These are not the 1960s. Today, not even the richest country on earth, the United States, could point to the moon and decree that, within a decade, an American would land on it. There is a deep distrust of government and politicians, a distrust born of the bitter experience of the 1970s and 1980s, when governments incurred deficits without being particularly effective.

People are rightly sceptical of big plans and grandiose schemes. All they generally want from government is simple competence. A step-by-step approach, solving one problem at a time, is the first stage in restoring a basic level of confidence and trust.

Woody Allen has been famously misquoted as saying that 90 percent of life is showing up. Perhaps this can be elevated to the Woody Allen Standard of Government: 90 percent involves being competent, caring, efficient, modest, prudent, and non-intrusive — in other words, just getting the job done. Indeed, if governments don't attend first to the overriding task of achieving simple competence, they really have no business launching new ventures.

The Woody Allen Standard can generally be attained by a well-trained, professional civil service supported by honest, career politicians. But hitting the standard presupposes a static, non-dynamic model of politics and human behaviour. It fails to take into account systemic change, unanticipated developments, or unprecedented situations.

It is in the realm of the 10 percent where the real action takes place. This is where the big problems, challenges, and opportunities lie. This is where the big changes have to be made, though that doesn't always mean downsizing, privatizing, and opting out. Sometimes, even these days, we have to build and create.

This 10 percent is what attracts outsiders to politics. Outsiders don't enter politics simply to administer things — that's why we have a civil service — they enter politics to change things. Not everything, of course, but a few big things. Outsiders see themselves as change agents, as strategists rather than transactionalists. They think outside the current assumptions of government because they think outside the system; they bring an outsider's perspective, something new to the party.

Traditional politicians worry excessively about polls. It would, of course, be political folly to ignore polls and the state of public opinion, but it is also the function of politicians to lead by informing people's opinions. What politicians, at their best, are supposed to do is develop ideas driven by a core set of beliefs. Those ideas are supposed, in turn, to form the policy agenda.

Finally, it is in the realm of the 10 percent where the politics of desire can be found. The Canada We Want can never be attained by politics as usual. If we want a Canada fit for the future, we need to think outside our current assumptions and current reality. Only National Projects, of the type described in the next four chapters, can take us where we want to be — to the Canada We Want.

6

A National Project on Developmental Health

"Canadian Doctors Take Their Talent South" ran the front-page headline in the *Globe and Mail* in July 1998. "Top doctors are moving to U.S. hospitals that offer unlimited research money and a chance to practice cutting-edge medicine. A Texas medical centre is a magnet for many," explained a subhead.

The story was about the University of Texas's MD Anderson Cancer Center, the busiest cancer hospital in North America. MD Anderson welcomes eighteen thousand new cancer patients from all over the world every year. It sees fifteen hundred patients every day in the outpatient clinic alone. And it has attracted fifteen Canadian physicians, including two brothers, Louis and Peter Pisters from London, Ontario.

The article made two main points. First, MD Anderson is far more richly funded than any Canadian centre; its annual budget of $170 million (Cdn.) compares with $48 million for the National Cancer Institute of Canada and $20 million for Toronto's Princess Margaret Hospital,

Canada's two largest cancer institutions. Second, it was a great loss to Canada that talented doctors like the Pisters brothers should feel obliged to leave the country to pursue their research.

Superficially, this was the story of an American success and a Canadian failure. But was this the real story? Lost in the admiring detail ("There is enough research space here to park 22 jumbo jets") was the fundamental question of whether this money was well spent. One Canadian doctor admitted that the number of patients cured by experimental therapies was "relatively low," and acknowledged that a point for debate was at what cost those lives were being extended.

Dr. Michele Donato, a McGill graduate, went to MD Anderson to launch an ambitious bone-marrow-transplant program to treat ovarian cancer, a disease that usually kills within five years. As Carolyn Abraham, the author of the article, noted, "No hard proof exists that transplants actually improve outcomes because few women with late-stage ovarian or breast cancer want to end up in a study's control group while the other group gets a transplant." When Abraham asked Dr. Donato why Canada should be expected to provide such costly treatments when there is no evidence that they work, the reply was "We'll never make progress if we think like that."

But perhaps the real answer is that we will never make progress if we think like the folks at MD Anderson. Of course, it all depends on how we choose to define "progress." Is it a better investment to spend prodigious amounts of money on new and unproved medical techniques for the initial marginal benefit of the very rich (a first consultation costs more than two thousand dollars, the most extravagant procedures a quarter of a million) and the very well-insured? Or should we consider an actual improvement in people's health to be a better indication of progress?

The MD Anderson story highlights a paradox. Here is the United States, the richest country in the world, spending huge amounts of money on a few patients to advance procedures with dubious results. At the same time, the U.S. has a population whose health status — when measured by longevity, infant-mortality rates, and other indicators — is significantly worse than that of the population of Canada, the country that is losing doctors to MD Anderson and spending considerably less of its GNP on health care.

Most advanced countries in the world are experiencing a perceived crisis in their health care systems. This crisis stems from the fact that no society has the resources to meet the ever-growing demands and "unmet needs" of a modern health care system. How many MD Andersons can even the United States support?

More crucially, there is no evidence that there is any connection between the amount of money we spend on health care and how healthy we are as a population. As Canadian health economists Robert Evans and Greg Stoddard have brilliantly demonstrated in their essay "Producing Health, Consuming Health Care," in *Why Are Some People Healthy and Others Not?* (1994), "The growing field of health services research has accumulated extensive evidence inconsistent with the assumption that the provision of health care is connected in any systematic or scientifically grounded way with patient 'needs' or demonstrable outcomes. . . . Accordingly, the greatly increased flow of resources into health care is perceived as not having a commensurate, or in some cases any, impact on health status. Nor is there any demonstrable connection between international variations in health status and variations in health spending."

Japan offers the most vivid proof that expenditures on health care have no connection to improved health. While Americans are currently spending about 14 percent of their GNP on health care, the Japanese have for years been spending no more than 7 percent. Yet even though Japan had, in 1960, one of the lowest rates of life expectancy of any of the developed nations, the country led the world in life expectancy by 1990, gaining, on average, six years on Americans during the same period.

So if there is little or no connection between health expenditures and health status, two related questions arise: what *is* the purpose of a health care system if it isn't to improve the overall health status of the population; and how *can* we improve our health if spending more money on health care won't do it?

As has often been said, the purpose of the health care system isn't to promote health, it's to deal with sickness. It should more properly be referred to as a "sickness care system." As Evans and Stoddard have noted, "Health care . . . is overwhelmingly *reactive* in nature, responding to perceived departures from health, and identifying those departures in terms of clinical concepts and categories: diseases, professionally defined. The definition of health implicit in (most of) the behaviour of the health care system, the collection of people and institutions involved in the provision of care, is a negative concept: the absence of disease or injury."

There is nothing wrong or demeaning in describing the sickness care system this way. Dealing with sick people is a supremely important activity. And there is no doubt that medical science has, in the words of Evans and Stoddard, "enhanced our ability to prevent some diseases, cure others, and alleviate the symptoms or slow the progress of many more." Yet, as the World Health Organization noted more than forty years ago in its classic definition of the word "health," "Health is a state of complete physical, mental, and social well-being, and not merely the absence of disease or injury." Thus the formulation of a *health* policy would be a far more profound and far-ranging enterprise than simply dealing with sickness and injury.

The problem, according to Evans and Stoddard, has been that because the health care industry is one of the largest clusters of economic activity in all modern states, *care* policy has dominated *health* policy. The purpose of this chapter is to unbundle these two distinct concepts, health care and health, to see what a new National Project on health might look like, and to understand how our existing National Project on health care could be modified to make a greater contribution to the health of Canadians.

HEALTH

The World Health Organization's definition of the positive aspects of health ("a state of complete physical, mental, and social well-being") is a rich, powerful, and challenging one in terms of its public policy implications. How on earth, for example, can societies improve the likelihood of people experiencing "social well-being"? What aspect of human life, public or private, would not be implicated in such an enterprise? And how can a society create a National Project with such a vast and lofty ambition?

The answer may lie partly in the pioneering work of a group of researchers associated with the Human Development Program of the Canadian Institute for Advanced Research. In the introductory chapter of *Developmental Health and the Wealth of Nations*, a new book edited by Daniel Keating and Clyde Hertzman, the editors posit an idea called developmental health, a refinement of the traditional notion of health.

In effect, Keating and Hertzman take the World Health Organization's concept of health and make it dynamic rather than static. They move the WHO's definition ("a state of complete physical, mental, and social well-being") through time, seeing it as a continuous developmental process from womb to tomb, from sperm to worm. Hence, the term "developmental health," which covers a range of developmental outcomes, including not only physical and mental health, but also such indicators as behavioural adjustment, literacy, and mathematical achievement.

At first glance it is difficult to see why a definition of health that seems even more wide-ranging and inclusive than the already ambitious definition of the World Health Organization would lead us to a clearer sense of public policy options. But as the title of the book suggests, the concept of developmental health can be linked to the wealth of nations. Paradoxically, the appropriate economic response of the nation-state to the challenges of globalization may reside in an expanded view of health policy, which we may choose to call a National Project on Developmental Health.

Keating and Hertzman begin their argument with what they call modernity's paradox. On the one hand, globalization has led to a dramatic expansion of market-based economies, which have generated far more wealth than at any previous time in history. On the other hand, the health and well-being of children and youth are far more threatened by the forces of social change today than in the past. Social disruptions such as unemployment or a lack of adequate child care threaten not only the families of the poor, but also the children of moderately secure families. As a result, Keating and Hertzman's central concern is "whether today's children and youth are developing in a positive and healthy way, and how we might deal with the impact of rapid social and technological change on society's ability to support human development."

Keating and Hertzman lay out three big concepts whose interconnections have profound consequences for a National Project on Developmental Health: populations and gradients, the biological "embedding" of gradients in early development, and the economic consequences of developmental health. Let's look at each of these three concepts in detail.

Populations and Gradients

A gradient is simply a tilted line, like the angle of a road rising over a hill. The steeper the angle of the hill, the steeper the gradient of the road.

A socio-economic gradient for health status is simply a tilted line which shows that there is a direct relation between how well off we are economically and socially and how healthy we are. At the lower end of the gradient are the poorest people with the worst health; at the upper end are the richest people with the best health. A crucial point of the argument is that the gradient is continuous, without breaks, meaning that the entire population can be found somewhere along the tilted line. It is not simply that poor people are sicker; it is that with every increase in socio-economic status, there is a commensurate improvement in health for all members of society.

Since we are all on the gradient, a discussion about improving health outcomes should address more than the elimination of poverty; it should be a discussion about flattening the gradient in such a way that all of us can be healthier.

There is also a corresponding socio-economic gradient in human development, with the poorest people having the least chance of developing to their full potential and the richest people the best. When you add the two socio-economic gradients together, you have an overall socio-economic gradient for developmental health.

What is the significance of these gradients? Keating and Hertzman explain: "We start here because the evidence leads us to believe that the steepness of these gradients gives important clues as to whether a society is supporting or undermining the development of its population. Most significant is the finding that for all areas of developmental health, steep gradients are associated with overall poorer outcomes in comparisons among countries or regions. In particular, steep gradients together with lower levels of developmental health suggest a society is failing as a collective entity, or that it is in a disruptive social transition due to technological, economic, or political change."

The authors note that we routinely make important policy decisions based on economic and environmental impact analyses. "The fact that we do not have any systematic way of evaluating the human development impact of the choices we make in the public sector, in the private sector, and in communities, is an indicator that we have not fully grasped the crucial point that these aspects of human development are central not only to our current well-being but also to our future prospects as a society."

Research into gradients has uncovered three sets of "big facts." First, in wealthy societies, the greater the inequities in income distribution, the poorer the overall health status of the population. Second, there is direct relationship between the steepness of the income gradient and the steepness of the socio-economic gradient for health status. Conversely, the more gradual the socio-economic gradient for health status, the higher the overall level of health in a society. In other words, our health status may have as much to do with what kind of a society we live in as it does with our individual characteristics. For example, Sweden is a country with a gradual income gradient, and not only is the overall health status of the population significantly higher than in Britain, which has steeper income gradients, but Swedes at the lower end of the income gradient live longer than Britons at the higher end.

Finally, socio-economic gradients in health status can be found in different historical eras with different diseases. In one era, tuberculosis was a major killer, as cancer is today. People of lower socio-economic status in any era are more likely to die earlier of whatever disease is dominant. Socio-economic gradients in health status can be found across a wide range of diseases, including those with and without a behavioural component, such as smoking-induced lung cancer.

At this point in the argument, a crucial question arises: Is the socio-economic gradient for developmental health entirely dependent on the distribution of income and wealth in a society? If the answer is yes, the public policy implications might seem simple: flatten the income gradients through a more aggressive tax regime. But although the evidence certainly points in that direction, Keating and Hertzman suggest that the story is more complex, speculating that there are other "nurturing" processes that also affect socio-economic gradients.

If socio-economic gradients vary across national or regional groups that have comparable levels of wealth and income inequality, the possibility arises that they vary in their distributions of "developmental nurturance". Factors such as education, or stable communities, or stable families, or the opportunities for youth to participate in meaningful activities may be driven by other social processes besides income. In other words, the social goods of nurturance might not be distributed in an identical way to the distribution of wealth in a given society. This is a very important question to consider, because it may suggest a range of developmentally effective social actions and policies beyond wealth distribution.

One way of using information about gradients to inform social policy is to measure outcomes to identify groups of individuals, schools, and communities that are outperforming the socio-economic gradient. If we can then discover how these groups or communities managed collectively to improve the quality of their social environments, we may be able to share this knowledge with other communities as well as with policy-makers.

In summary, then, the argument about gradients and their relation to health suggests that the distribution of material or social goods has a far greater and more measurable impact on developmental health than health care expenditures per capita. Therefore, if we are serious about improving the health of nations, we should spend at least as much time thinking about the policy implications of income distribution and at least as much money investing in the quality of our social environments as we spend thinking about and investing in health care.

Biological Embedding

Biological embedding is the key link between human development and health. It is also the transmission belt by which socio-economic factors affect our health.

Central to the notion of biological embedding is the concept of critical periods in early development. Keating and Hertzman define "critical periods" as "periods during which the experiences of the organism will be encoded, especially in the neural system. Before and after critical periods, the same experience will have little or no effect on the developing organism. The existence of such critical periods increases the likelihood that biological embedding may be a key feature of the observed population patterns in developmental health."

During these critical periods, the brain is "sculpted" by external experiences. Both the immune system and the hormone system are affected by the brain's reaction to outside events. The first months of a child's life are crucial. If, instead of the human warmth and nurturing that builds the trust and confidence necessary for a baby to experiment, learn, and grow, there is a lack of affection, or worse, violence, the immune system will be constantly aroused in response to perceived danger. The brain will be programmed to respond to the outside world with wariness, not trust, and it will be increasingly difficult for the child to develop normal attachments to other people and to feel self-confident enough to try and fail and try again. In other words, negative external experiences "wire" the brain negatively during a critical period of development, with the potential for lifelong consequences.

Because socio-economic gradients correlate with the kinds of family environments likely to produce negative or positive effects on young children, our failure as a society to attend to the importance of flattening the gradient and improving family environments has long-term negative social and economic consequences for all of us.

Keating and Hertzman explain that there are particularly sensitive periods in the development of the systems that regulate emotions, attention spans, and social responses. Events that occur in the first year of life can affect the ability of people to function well as they enter the first grade of school. The existence of gradients in the population reflects these developmental processes that occur at the individual level. Biology may provide the crucial explanation for complex patterns of population effects on human development.

The Virtuous Circle of Economic Growth and Developmental Health

Earlier, we noted the remarkable improvement in the longevity of the Japanese over the past forty years; this improvement is all the more remarkable in light of their relatively modest investment in health care spending. Many explanations have been proffered, but they all fail to provide the answer. There were no outstanding breakthroughs in medical science; the physical environment did not become less crowded or polluted; diets do not seem to have changed radically.

Instead, we are left with the extraordinary hypothesis that it was economic growth itself and the way in which the Japanese both contributed to and equitably benefited from those high rates of growth that led to improved health outcomes. As Evans and Stoddard have noted, this change was not simply the result of a rise in disposable incomes; it may have had more to do with the greatly enhanced sense of individual and collective self-worth, and with a renewed hope for the future, which both characterized and accompanied their economic growth. "A number of observers, concerned not with comparative health status but with international economic competitiveness, have noted the extraordinary Japanese sense of self-confidence and pride arising from their rapid progress toward economic world leadership," they explain. "Individually and as a nation, the Japanese are seeing themselves as harder-working, brighter, richer, and just plain better than the rest of the world. Could this attitude be yielding health benefits as well?"

In the case of Japan, there seems to be a positive relationship between a societal commitment to economic growth and a more equitable distribution of its rewards on the one hand, and a resulting increased sense of collective self-worth and improved health on the other. But the converse is also true: healthier, better-developed people are more able to contribute to a growing economy. If the key characteristic of globalization is the rapidity of the rate of external change to which countries and people must respond, then the quality of our people — their flexibility, ingenuity, willingness to adapt, and ability to cope with change — becomes the crucial factor for success. Hence, the investments we make in developmental health become our most significant economic investments.

Keating and Hertzman use the term "learning societies" to describe those communities that provide the essential supports for developmental health by drawing on existing material, cultural, and social resources in a purposeful way. Learning societies have the capacity for timely adaptation in the face of rapid social and technological change. Within such societies, it is the ability of individual communities to respond to these challenges through the creative organization of everyday social practices that means the difference between success and failure.

An economic cost-benefit analysis of the advantages of appropriate investments in developmental health would contain three elements. First, there is the cost of failing to make the investment, which results in reduced school performance, increased antisocial behaviour, and eventually reduced work participation.

Second, there are the converse benefits that come from the early investments that prevent these problems. There is an extensive literature on the advantages of head-start programs and high-quality early child care and education; this indicates a return of at least double the original investment in terms of all children, and as much as seven dollars saved for every one dollar invested for the most vulnerable and at-risk children. Society, in turn, can reinvest those savings in more productive ways, just as the Japanese were able to reinvest the money they saved by having lower health care costs than the Americans in increased economic productive capacity.

Third, there are the lost opportunities for economic growth if we fail to produce a population that is confident, innovative, and flexible. We often talk about productivity in such discussions, but at the heart of the productivity debate there are two basic elements: the quality of the population, and the ability of that population to organize itself collectively into a learning society.

Taken together, these economic arguments constitute a virtuous circle. The sooner we get on with making the requisite investments in developmental health, the sooner the positive consequences will be seen in improved health and developmental outcomes. The sooner the population is better developed and healthier, the sooner the savings will come in the health care system and other social support systems because of reduced demand. The sooner a healthier and better-developed population produces higher rates of economic growth, the sooner that population's sense of collective self-esteem rises and the sooner further improvements in health will follow.

But the only way to organize such investments and to mobilize existing resources at both the national and the community levels is to create a learning society that is flexible enough to adjust its social policies and investments in light of constantly changing circumstances. A learning society, in turn, would have the adaptive capacity and the "social capital," in Robert Putnam's phrase, to work on the solutions to the other major challenges faced by our societal systems: the environment, energy, transportation, culture, new media, and so forth.

A NATIONAL PROJECT ON DEVELOPMENTAL HEALTH

A National Project on Developmental Health might thus as easily be called a National Project to Create a Learning Society. In other words, the way in which we undertake such a project is as important as the project itself, because, like human development, learning is continuous, and a learning society worthy of the name would be constantly adapting and changing.

So where do we begin such an undertaking? To start, we have to be comfortable with this new theory of developmental health and its core dynamics. To be comfortable with the theory, we have to make sure it is right, which means that we have to fund the research, undertake experiments, and monitor the results. Keating and Hertzman identify some key guidelines to the core dynamics of human development.

First, the best results for social investments are likely to come from concentrating them at the natural human developmental transition periods: in the first few years of life; at school entry; at the transition to adolescence; at the transition to adulthood.

Second, the constant monitoring of our efforts is necessary to detect problems early on. This feedback loop allows learning to occur and corrective action to be taken. "In blunt terms, we need to learn how to keep score. This is not only in comparisons between similar communities, but also in comparisons within communities across time. We should be routinely asking whether we are doing better this year than last year, on reliable indicators of population developmental health, like readiness to learn as children enter school, or rates of anti-social behaviour or delinquency."

Finally, we need to be constantly alert to the external changes, be they technological, demographic, or economic, that shift the equations and challenge our basic operating assumptions. By definition, the contexts within which we function, and hence the ways in which we work to support developmental health, are dynamic. We need to be flexible and responsive to any changes, which means that programs and services may have to be altered over time to reflect new realities, whether those realities are an ageing population, new information technologies, or indeed, new understandings of how the world works.

We also need to be able to tap into our existing medical research base to incorporate these new understandings on developmental health. One promising initiative comes from Toronto's Hospital for Sick Children, which has created the Community Health Systems Resource Group. The group fully accepts the broader context of the determinants of health and believes that a systems-based approach to understanding health requires the coordination, cooperation, and commitment of all sectors. It also understands the importance of evidence-based interventions that effect and sustain behavioural change, which in turn improves functioning at the family and community levels.

The mission of the group is to create "more resilient children in more resilient families in more resilient communities," a philosophy that is entirely consistent with the wider objectives of a National Project on Developmental Health. What is particularly important about this initiative is that it ties the traditional health care community to a larger project which stresses that there are a variety of interventions, including, but not limited to, health care, which need to be woven together to improve developmental health outcomes, and that all these interventions and outcomes need to be measured in a standardized, rigorous, and system-wide fashion.

SHARING THE THEORY: THE IMPORTANCE OF SOCIAL LEARNING

By shifting the terms of debate from "getting the health care system right" to "getting people healthier," we are presenting an enormous challenge to both conventional wisdom and deeply entrenched interests. After all, every dollar that is invested in the wider determinants of developmental health is a dollar that might have gone to a drug company, or a doctor, or a hospital, or an advanced biomedical research centre like MD Anderson.

This shift is doubly difficult to make at a time when there is a perceived funding crisis in the health care system. When people are sick, when emergency rooms are crowded, when waiting lists are long, when doctors take flight south, the last thing an anxious public wants or needs to hear is that if we'd done the right thing twenty years ago, we wouldn't be in this pickle now. And yet, if we don't begin to make the shift now, we will never begin to "solve" the health care crisis. We will always be trapped between spiralling demand, decreasing resources, and an ever-grumpier public (whose very grumpiness may even be a source of subsequent ill health!).

Our challenge is to involve our fellow citizens in the discussion, not simply by making the case in all available forums, from the education system to the media, but by constructing consultative mechanisms to involve as many people as possible in sharing the new information and working through its policy implications. This is where the role of civil society is so important. It is not enough for policy wonks to agree. It is not even enough if politicians and bureaucrats are brought on board. Unless there is understanding and buy-in from the broader public, unless there is a constituency for these new ideas, the requisite policies will never be implemented.

In July 1998, the Canadian Council on Social Development released a paper entitled "Talking with Canadians: Citizen Engagement and the Social Union," which chronicles some of the experiences and successes Canadians have enjoyed in the area of social learning and citizen engagement. The paper contrasts "public consultation and participation," which is basically "telling and selling" the public about programs, with "engagement," which economist Judith Maxwell describes as a process whereby citizens are asked to reflect on choices and trade-offs involving conflicts of values or difficult resource allocation decisions.

Why is citizen engagement more powerful than citizen consultations? "First, citizen engagement holds out the promise of significant or 'real' influence upon public policy decisions. . . . The second difference is that citizen engagement is more likely to have a positive and lasting effect on civil society and social cohesion. Through sustained participation involving deliberation and learning, people may acquire the skills of citizenship, clarify their own values, better appreciate and tolerate the views of others and change their own behaviour. . . . At the broader level, the development of community capacity can lead to action."

The authors proceed to analyze various examples of citizen engagement, including two Quebec summits on the economy and social development, the Alberta Growth Summit, the Hamilton-Wentworth Constituent Assembly, and the National Forum on Health. They find the last to be the most instructive, explaining that the process engaged citizens in discussions of fundamental values, as well as policy and program options arising from a broader understanding of the non-medical determinants of health. Participants in the forum were able to see the relationship between local concerns and national policy considerations. As a result, the forum has had a major impact on such developments as the federal Health Transition Fund, which sponsors local and regional experiments in population health.

The National Forum on Health has been successful in focusing the attention of the government on both the broader determinants of health and the importance of outcomes-based research, and it has a track record in citizen engagement. It might be appropriate to ask the forum to broaden its work to support both the research and social-learning aspects of a National Project on Developmental Health.

CREATING A NETWORK FOR A NATIONAL PROJECT ON DEVELOPMENTAL HEALTH

Assuming that we have the theory straight, and that the requisite social learning has ensued, we then have to do the actual hard work. The first problem is figuring out who "we" is. The rhetorical answer, of course, is "all of us," but that doesn't get us very far. Someone has to call the meeting.

This is the traditional function of political leadership in the most inspired sense: we elect people to look after the interests of all society, of all our citizens. The problem is that the concept of developmental health is so all-encompassing that traditional government structures can't handle it. Keating and Hertzman describe the gap between government as we know it and a learning organization:

> One of the hallmarks of learning organizations essential to a learning society is the ability to network the available resources in order to maximize the benefits of our efforts. What we often discover, however, is that the coordination among public and private organizations which provide developmental resources is minimal or absent altogether. This has often been described as the "silo effect," in which each of the organizations — education, health, community and social services, juvenile justice, the voluntary sector — is structured vertically, with a head office of some sort and a bureaucratic structure which ensures that members of the organization look toward the centre for resources and for direction. This usually creates barriers to effective cooperation at the local level, where a given child or family confronts a Byzantine array of services or activities which are almost impossible to comprehend, much less use effectively.

So how do we take a country like Canada, with all of its nineteenth-century constitutional quirkiness, and turn it into a learning organization fit for the twenty-first century and capable of undertaking a monumental National Project on Developmental Health?

In October 1994, the federal Department of Finance released its so-called purple book (purple because it was a combination of red and blue, as wags noted at the time), *A New Framework for Economic Policy*. Its author was the brilliant economic theorist Peter Nicholson, who was serving as an in-house guru and adviser to Paul Martin at the time. In the purple book, Nicholson offered two aphorisms on the future of government that may give us a hint as to how governments can help societies become learning organizations.

This was Nicholson's First Law: "The comparative advantage of government is knowledge." While the federal government may be forced by economic circumstance to limit its programs and expenditures, it should never lose its capacity to be the centre for all knowledge of what is happening in the country. This is not to be confused with a totalitarian state, however, whose purpose is to know everything about everyone in the country. Rather, the federal government, through its own research capability, its own information systems, its own networking capacity, should be the primary source of knowledge about the country. At the very least, the government should know more than anyone else about what is happening in Canada, even if it may not have the resources to do a whole lot with that knowledge.

That is why it is crucial that organizations like Statistics Canada, the National Research Council, the Medical Research Council, the Social Sciences and Humanities Research Council, and the Natural Sciences and Engineering Research Council be well funded. That is why it made enormous sense for Industry Canada to create Strategis, an Internet website that is the definitive source for statistical business information in Canada. That is why, as will be discussed in a later chapter, it is so important for the federal government to invest heavily in establishing Canada's presence in new media, both domestically and internationally.

In practical terms, this means that for a National Project on Developmental Health to be successful, the first task of the federal government is to fund, collect, and disseminate research in the theory of developmental health. Government must be in the forefront of funding experiments, prototypes, and pilot projects to test the new theory. Government must also facilitate the monitoring of outcomes so that it is better able to adjust its own programs and practices accordingly. In short, government must be the intelligent repository of all relevant information on the subject of developmental health, or at least, like a good librarian, know who else's library might have the book.

Which brings us to Nicholson's Second Law: "The new metaphor for government is the network." In an age of restrained spending, no one government can do it all. Therefore, every government is obliged to work with other governments and with civil society if it intends to undertake any great project.

This seeming fiscal disadvantage carries with it two virtues. First, for areas like developmental health and the environment, which do not lend themselves to single-department, single-government "silo" solutions, being forced by economic circumstance to work with partners in a networked manner is actually a good thing, provided we are all singing from the same theoretical song sheet. Second, if part of the challenge of mounting a National Project is finding appropriate instruments for citizen participation and social learning, the network approach probably has a greater chance of ultimate success than the more traditional approach of having Caesar Augustus send the word down.

So who calls the meeting to get a National Project on Developmental Health going? Certainly those organizations and researchers who have some interest and expertise in the matter can call on governments to do something, but ultimately, since the question is clearly of national importance, it is the federal government that has to issue the challenge, provisionally set the goal, invite the partners, and launch the network. Even in recent memory, there are examples of the federal government doing precisely that: when it created the National Forum on Health, for example, or the National Tourism Commission, or the Team Canada trade missions.

Indeed, the building blocks of a National Project on Developmental Health are already in place. The initial "missionary" work was done by the Ontario Premier's Councils, first under David Peterson, then under Bob Rae, both of whom collaborated extensively with the team of pioneering researchers clustered around the Canadian Institute for Advanced Research (CIAR). More recently, there has been the continuing work of the National Forum on Health and the promising activities of the National Children's Agenda, which will be discussed in more detail in the next chapter. Even the current discussions on renewing the social union have the potential to lead to some creative networked solutions to major national problems, provided the participants can abandon the rhetoric of provincial rights and autonomy, put aside the antiquated notion that all problems have to be solved exclusively by one order of government or the other, and focus on allowing the structure of the problem to dictate the structure of the solution.

In short, Canadian society has to become a learning organization, with governments leading the way. In such an organization, dusty constitutional considerations have to take a back seat to the imperative of the problem.

It is important to note, as Keating and Hertzman do, that effective participation in a network, a National Project, a learning organization, a collaborative effort does not depend on a uniformity of goals among all the partners. They explain that for those who labour under this misconception,

> it is easy to dismiss the notion of an effective learning organization (or learning society) merely by taking note of the prevalence of conflict and competition in human activity. From this view, the only route to effective collaborative learning or action is to impose

uniformity from some central source. The heart of this misconception is the view that competition and cooperation are exclusive states. It can be observed in many well-functioning complex systems that cooperation and competition are linked in a dynamic tension which is essential to the system's functioning. . . . Indeed, an essential component of a learning organization is the assurance that valuable information is not lost to the system due to internal conflict, and thus competing views need to be encouraged and heard.

In our chapter on children, we describe in detail how one aspect of a National Project on Developmental Health might initially be undertaken. A full-blown National Project on Developmental Health would in some ways be the aggregate of a series of sub-projects of this sort, including some of those discussed in subsequent chapters. The organizational challenge is to weave these various projects together in a purposeful way that would produce maximum synergies, while still retaining the overall flexibility characteristic of true learning organizations. To this end, we might be able to learn from the Australian forum for intergovernmental decision-making, the Council of Australian Governments (COAG).

In a 1996 paper entitled "Building Blocks for Canada's New Social Union," Margaret Biggs, a federal social policy analyst, describes in some detail the Australian experience and its relevance for Canada. COAG, she explains, grew out of annual premiers' meetings, but has a more ambitious policy-making and decision-making mandate. Initiatives can come from either level of government, and the style and substance of meetings is cooperative and collaborative, with substantial negotiations and policy-making taking place. She goes on to say, "What distinguishes COAG from the Ministerial Council system is that it addresses areas of national significance and has a central agency, 'whole of government' perspective. COAG is a forum for spearheading reform, challenging existing processes and thinking, and making the cross-sectoral linkages and trade-offs that are often essential to a 'national' solution."

One of the great (and relevant) achievements of COAG has been to evaluate the outcomes, not just the outputs, of public administration at both governmental levels in Australia. This entailed developing national performance indicators across a wide range of sectors, and it required a high degree of collaboration to put in place. "And probably the most salient insight for Canada is how an intergovernmental body like COAG can provide a national forum to address national-level issues and interests, and how national solutions need not be centrally imposed or controlled," remarks Biggs. "This had been accomplished without creating a new level of government and bureaucracy."

SO WHAT WOULD WE ACTUALLY DO?

Assuming we could get the theory right, assuming we could put in place appropriate mechanisms for social learning, and assuming we could create an appropriate network and learning organization to pull all of us together for the common cause of advancing developmental health, then what would we do? Keating and Hertzman suggest some obvious policy directions that arise from their theory of how developmental health is actually produced.

First, Canadians will have to recognize that there now exists an almost total mismatch between where society currently makes its greatest social investments and where those investments would be most effective. Clearly, we have seriously underinvested in human development between conception and school age because there is an unconscious assumption in our institutional arrangements that early development is the least important stage, not the most. This is why there has been a net transfer of wealth towards older people from younger families with children. This is why societies invest so heavily in institutions for grown-ups, like universities, hospitals, and prisons, and so little in institutions for kids, like high-quality public daycare. The obvious policy solution is to redress the balance, starting with rethinking our abiding obsession with increasing health care funding.

Second, if we are to begin to reinvest more heavily in healthy child development, we need to understand what the key elements of that development are: income, nutrition, child care, stimulation, love and support, advocacy, and safety. In practical terms, we need to address the tremendous strains that contemporary society places on families. Labour market changes, increased mobility, and a decline in community coherence all need to be at least partially offset by things like stable, high-quality child care.

Third, we need to recognize, as Keating and Hertzman do, that continuing to collect "evidence of systematic variation in cognitive and behavioural development across communities and understanding its determinants is crucial for positive social change."

Finally, if developmental health depends on factors above and beyond flattening the income gradient, we need to look at the institutions of "social nurturance" — the family, the school, the neighbourhood, the community — to see how they can all be strengthened as part of our national network.

THE ROLE OF COMMUNITIES

The final challenge for our National Project is to create a nationwide structure that allows and encourages much of the action on developmental health to take place at the community level.

Keating and Hertzman see communities as the building blocks of a learning society, because communities can provide the social supports that go beyond income gradients in producing developmental health. The challenge for communities is to get past the silo effect of organizations like governments, whose efforts are frequently uncoordinated at the community level. "What is required is better strategic thinking which encourages local networks among those who provide developmental resources, whether in the service-delivery or the community-development sector."

Different communities need different approaches to achieve the same result. These distinct approaches reflect local circumstances, problems, and resources, which have to be configured. One size will most emphatically not fit all. "This is a planning process, not unlike community economic development, which entails the participation of many sectors and a realistic accounting of assets and liabilities of the community in promoting developmental health," explain Keating and Hertzman. "Moreover, the active participation of the whole community in such activities is in itself important in establishing community engagement and design and in monitoring the outcomes of the efforts."

What is the role of the federal and provincial governments in encouraging and assisting communities in this work? First, they are to provide communities with the resources to mobilize around a given task, as we will see in our next chapter with the Community Action Program for Children. Second, they are to obey Nicholson's two laws: tie local communities into the national knowledge base by making requisite information available, and gather information at the community level about local efforts and outcomes; then link the communities with each other and all the other partners in the National Project by taking advantage of the interactive potential of the Internet. Local communities can be a tremendous source of social nurturance when encouraged by the larger national community. Conversely, we undermine the competence of communities at our peril.

In November 1998 the *Globe and Mail*'s Toronto columnist John Barber described what can happen when communities are disempowered by government. "I am leaning against a folding table in an overcrowded meeting hall, listening to my neighbours scream at one another. They are going at it mercilessly, saying horrible things, inflicting wounds that could easily last a generation," he wrote. "They want to know why the bureaucrats selected a shuttered hospital on a residential street in their neighbourhood to function as an emergency winter shelter for Toronto's exploding population of homeless people."

Why the rage? It was not simply a result of the "not in my backyard" syndrome. Its more profound source was the powerlessness all the neighbours felt in the face of government decisions over which they had no control. A city bureaucrat attempted to explain: "In 1992, the federal government cancelled its social housing programs. In 1995, the provincial government cancelled its social housing programs."

Barber went on to observe:

The people are behaving badly, but I can't blame them. They have watched their neighbourhood deteriorate in complete helplessness, with the ruined people now almost piled up on the sidewalks. They have discovered they are equally helpless to influence the "solution" — the panicky human warehousing job that has become a rite of fall in Toronto.

I wonder how this happened, how the working-class immigrant families who are most upset about the prospect of a shelter ever became "part of the problem". They never elected anyone who promised to eliminate social programs and turn their neighbourhood into a human dumping ground. But that's what they got. This is the age of downloading, and the last thing to be loaded down is blame. It lands with a thud and makes an ugly mess.

What got destroyed that evening in Toronto was trust, mutual respect, affection, and the social capital that allows communities to do the right thing for their neighbours and to create an environment conducive to supporting developmental health. When we remove or diminish community resources like local schools because they fail to meet some mechanistic formula of square footage per child, when we fail to recognize the social glue that holds communities together, we are depleting a social asset.

When we diminish the control of communities over their local institutions, the gains we may make through centralized administration are far outweighed by the loss of a sense of involvement, ownership, and even responsibility for those institutions. And that loss of control, that sense of powerlessness and frustration, ultimately translates into worse developmental health outcomes for everyone in the community.

ENVOI

A National Project on Developmental Health is the most ambitious of all the National Projects, is, indeed, the Mother of all National Projects, since it will nurture the others. It represents the sum total of all our National Projects, because each one that succeeds will contribute in turn to our collective developmental health. And our ability to create a learning society through this project will be the measure of our ability to create all other National Projects.

Truly, the health of nations is the wealth of nations.

1

A National Project
for Canada's Children

In his 1996 budget, Paul Martin, Canada's finance minister, spoke of rekindling the national dream:

> The issue is, why can we not decide together in the House and in the country that ten years hence, Canada will be regarded as a world leader in the new industries of the new economy, in biotechnology, in environmental technology, in the cultural industries of the multichannel universe? Why not decide that ten years hence, increasing child poverty rates will be a thing of the past, that illiteracy will be erased from our communities, and that when it comes to international tests, our students will not simply do fine work but in fact will be the best?
>
> Why can we not decide together that medicare, ten years hence, will not simply survive, but be the most successful system in the world, a system that is second to none? Why not decide that ten years

hence our streets will be the safest they can be, not because we have the largest number of prisons or police, but because we have faced squarely the causes of crime?

Why not indeed?

The finance minister's list of goals was impressive, and we have chosen several of them as major themes of this book. But of those we have chosen as potential National Projects, one stands out above all others in its long-term strategic effect of fundamentally improving the lives of all Canadians.

The goal of that National Project would be to make Canada the best country in the world for the care and nurturing of young children. If we could say that Canada had the best prenatal programs, the lowest child poverty rates, the best parenting centres and parenting courses, the lowest rates of child abuse, and the best early childhood care and education programs, all of which culminated in the best rates of school readiness by age six, the positive consequences for Canada would be enormous.

With this single National Project, we will go a long way towards achieving many of the goals set out by Paul Martin. Not only will we reduce child poverty, we will also dramatically improve literacy rates, creating a solid base for future economic growth, and for employment success in the new economy.

Furthermore, if we produce six-year-olds with the best coping and learning skills in the world, this will eventually translate into improved adult health status (and hence reduce the need for health care). And fewer of these same six-year-olds will subsequently drop out, become delinquent, or commit crimes as they grow older.

What would be required to achieve such a National Project? Nothing less than a mobilization of all of our resources: parents and families, professionals and volunteers, public sector and private, community by community, province by province, coast to coast to coast. But by reconfiguring all of our existing assets around a central theory of what is needed for healthy early human development; by setting goals, objectives, and timelines; by measuring and monitoring our progress; by sharing best practices and results nationally and internationally through the Internet; and by encouraging each level of government and each sector of society to assume its share, this National Project is eminently achievable.

Why not indeed?

SO WHERE DO WE BEGIN?

We must begin with a mission statement. We could do worse than to borrow and adapt the goal set by the Early Years Action Group of North York, which is now part of the mega-city of Toronto: "To ensure that every child in Canada is 'ready to learn' at entrance to formal school education."

Why would we choose this mission statement? Because, in the words of the North York group, "This condition requires that the primary needs common to all children, and the additional special needs of some, have been met from conception to six years. The child is then cognitively, emotionally, socially and physically ready to learn according to individual potential."

But why the compelling need for this particular project? The answer lies partially in how well (or poorly) Canadian children are doing without it. A few stark facts make the case. First, according to *The Progress of Canada's Children*, a 1997 report by the Canadian Council on Social Development, the number of children living below the poverty line rose to 1.47 million in 1995 from 1.36 million in 1994, bringing the proportion of poor children under the age of eighteen to 21 percent from 19.5 percent. Second, according to the National Longitudinal Survey of Children and Youth, 5.7 percent of all children in Canada have low birth weight, which, in turn, is the source of two-thirds of all infant mortality. Third, the United Way notes that of the 2.5 million Canadian children under the age of six, more than 20 percent are known to be at risk of developing serious health, disability, or behavioural problems; 40 percent of Canada's children come to school in an unfit state to learn; 23 percent of three- and four-year-olds have been found to be seriously aggressive; and 71 percent of seriously aggressive six-year-olds grow into violent, anti-social adults.

How would a National Project address these and other challenges of the sort issued by the finance minister? The answer lies in our enhanced understanding of the human development story, particularly as it relates to the early development of the brain.

In June 1998, the House of Commons Standing Committee on Human Resources Development and the Status of Persons with Disabilities held a four-hour round-table discussion called "Children Prenatal to Six — Readiness to Learn." Members of the committee heard from a number of experts, including Dr. Fraser Mustard, founder of the Canadian Institute for Advanced Research (CIAR), whose pioneering programs on population health and human development were mentioned in the previous chapter.

Mustard explained why the early period of brain development determines our basic competence and coping skills, as well as the learning, behavioural, and health risks to which we will be exposed for the rest of our lives. With the recent revolution in neuroscience, we now know that the billions of neurons we are all born with form connections, the so-called wiring of the brain, and that those connections are made and shaped by the nature and quality of our earliest experiences after birth. We perceive life through sensing pathways (sight, touch, smell, etc.), and it is through these pathways that love, nurturing, and everything else help form the connections in the brain. Thus the sensing pathways become very important in the hard-wiring of the brain, which subsequently affects such basic characteristics of human behaviour as attachment, emotional control and stability, and arousal patterns (fight or flight).

The critical period for the formation of these pathways is the first six years of life, particularly the late in utero period and the first three years. The core component of the brain — including the limbic system and the midbrain, which are coupled in, like a central switchboard, to all the information from our sensing pathways — probably gets wired in the first three years of life.

The significance of this is that young children brought up in environments where there is violence or physical or verbal abuse between the parents will actually be affected in the wiring of this core function of the brain. This leads to children who have very complex emotional and behavioural problems by the time they enter the school system.

We also know that indicators that measure how well the brain has developed during this period have substantial predictive power. One of these indicators measures a child's readiness to learn when he or she enters the school system. In the United States, readiness-to-learn indicators have been linked to grade eight math performance, and there is a perfect correlation: the states with the highest number of students heading into the school system ready to learn also have the best grade eight math-performance levels. Thus, as the author of the study, Dick Fuchs, said, if we really want to improve math performance, we have to invest in preschool.

The implications of this research are profound. As Fraser Mustard points out, economic growth in Canada is entirely dependent on the quality of our population. Thus early childhood development is a substantial economic issue for the future, because how well we handle the brain-development question now will determine the quality of our population and our workforce twenty years hence.

Mustard also notes the link between early childhood development and crime prevention. Quoting Montreal researcher Richard Tremblay's work on male juvenile delinquency, Mustard says that a high proportion (though not all) of the kids who hit the school system showing anti-social behaviour will drop out early, even though the schools intervene to try to turn things around. We also know that 30 percent of these children will be delinquent by the age of thirteen. So what we do in preschool is probably more important than encouraging these kids to stay in the school system and not be delinquent when they become teenagers.

There are also considerable negative costs when societies fail to make the needed investments in early childhood development. Subsidizing early childhood support, notes Daniel Keating, saves money down the road in areas like special education, juvenile correction services, and teen pregnancy. The less we invest earlier, the more the costs, both financial and social, build up later.

But the most important consideration is the impact of early childhood development on adult health status. Mustard, a physician, says, "These early events have huge effects on the chronic diseases of adult life: mental health problems, such as depression, and even my pet subject, coronary heart disease. Indeed, I could argue that an early childhood educator probably has more effect in preventing coronary heart disease than all the investments you can make in cholesterol-lowering drugs."

EARLY CHILDHOOD: THE ROLE OF THE FEDERAL GOVERNMENT

There is overwhelming evidence supporting the importance of investing in early childhood development. Thanks to the work of Fraser Mustard, his associates, and many others, this version of the early stages of the human development story has been widely accepted, not only by early childhood specialists, but also by increasing numbers of policy-makers, bureaucrats, members of the public, and even politicians. What, then, prevents us from moving forward as a society to make the necessary investments in an organized and coherent manner?

Plenty. To begin with, this, like the environment, is one of those typically messy problems of the late twentieth century that defies neat and tidy categorization and resolution. Let's start, for example, with a fundamental question: Whose job is it to take care of these early childhood investments? If we put aside the primary responsibility of parents, families, and communities, which level of government has the chief constitutional responsibility for the education, care, and nurturing of preschool children? The answer is far from clear. We know that school-age children have a much more direct connection with the provinces, because the provinces have formal constitutional responsibility for the school system. We know that post-secondary education is a grey area, with the provinces having primary jurisdiction but the federal government supporting universities indirectly through the Canadian Health and Social Transfer. The federal government has also established a role for itself supporting student access to higher education through loans and scholarships, as well as much of the research that takes place on university campuses.

But what of children younger than school age? Here, the constitutional picture is murky. The provinces are responsible for social services, including welfare, daycare, and institutions such as the Children's Aid Society, and they are also responsible for nursery schools. But the federal government has traditionally provided income support for children through the tax system, as well as through direct grants to families with programs like the old baby bonus.

Another form of federal assistance for children comes from the Department of Human Resources Development, which, by providing financial support through the new National Child Benefit, encourages lower-income Canadians to get off welfare and rejoin the workforce. The department also has a direct interest in the quality of Canada's future workforce, and has sponsored pilot projects on establishing readiness-to-learn indicators at the community level.

The federal Department of Justice is concerned with young offenders, and promotes crime prevention and early intervention as a means to reduce the later incidence of juvenile delinquency. Through the National Crime Prevention Centre, the Department of Justice works with communities to establish programs intended to reduce subsequent crime, and these programs may directly involve young children.

Aboriginal Canadians traditionally have a special relationship with the federal government, as do their children. The Department of Indian Affairs and Northern Development, working with the federal Department of Health, has developed specific programs, such as the Aboriginal Head Start

Program, for young aboriginal children both on and off the reserve.

But the department that offers by far the most compelling point of direct contact between the federal government and Canada's children is Health Canada. No one challenges the federal government's role in health promotion across the country. And now that we have indisputable evidence of the huge lifelong health benefits that accrue from proper early childhood development, Health Canada is well positioned to assume a leadership role on behalf of the entire federal government in promoting a National Project for Canada's children. Indeed, a number of the department's existing programs, including the Community Action Program for Children (CAPC), the Canada Prenatal Nutrition Program, and the Aboriginal Head Start program, are potential building blocks for the new National Project.

In total, there are no fewer than sixteen federal ministers with direct or indirect responsibility for children. They include the ministers of Finance; Health; Human Resources Development; Indian Affairs and Northern Development; Justice; Revenue; Citizenship and Immigration; Canadian Heritage; the Environment; Public Works, through the Canada Mortgage and Housing Corporation; Transport; International Cooperation, through the Canadian International Development Agency; and Foreign Affairs, as well as the Secretary of State for Children and Youth, the Secretary of State for the Status of Women, and the Solicitor General.

So what is holding the federal government back? The first challenge, as we have noted, is that issues relating to children, like those relating to technology or the environment, are contemporary cross-cutting issues that defy the old structures of government. Not only is there a problem sorting out the roles the different levels of government should play, there are also problems within each of those orders of government. As long as federal departments continue to function within their existing silos, it will be difficult for them to focus their efforts on children's needs, let alone mount a National Project involving other levels of government and sectors of society. And yet, when the federal Department of Justice creates an intervention program targeting children at risk, when Health Canada worries about children under the age of six, when Human Resources Development Canada tries to help at-risk children of the working poor, when the Department of Finance wants to give a tax break to poor families with children, when Indian Affairs and Northern Development creates a Head Start Program — often these programs are meant for exactly the same children. Clearly, not a lot can happen until the federal government gets its own act together when it comes to Canada's youngest citizens.

But there is an equally serious barrier to direct federal involvement in creating this National Project: a fundamental lack of vision and will. As noted before, this underlying problem is often explained away as a desire to avoid the reckless years of government overspending. It's far simpler to downsize, reduce government programs, download services to the provinces, and either return any surplus funds to the taxpayer or use them to pay down the existing accumulated debt. Without doubt, each of these strategies can be justified on a case-by-case basis. There were plenty of costly and inefficient federal government programs. There were unwarranted federal intrusions into fields of exclusive provincial jurisdiction. Taxpayers are heavily burdened. The federal debt is still too high. But for all that, these strategies are often a cover for some not-so-hidden agendas, as well as some traditionally Canadian challenges.

A FEW LITTLE PROBLEMS

First, the not-so-hidden agendas. Because we live in an era dominated by talk of free markets and reduced government intervention, and because we have been forced to reduce government expenditures thanks to our previously foolish fiscal ways, there is a significant contingent of Canadians who believe that the only sane route lies in tax cuts and further cuts to government spending. This contingent counts among its ranks members of the Reform Party, the Conservative parties of Alberta and Ontario as well as the national PCs, and some members of the federal and provincial Liberal parties.

Such people have basically lost faith in the ability of governments to govern and societies to conduct their own affairs. Like Ian Angell, they would have us believe that the forces of the market and of globalization are irresistible, that the only rules of the game are those devised by the Ronald Thatcherites who dominated Western economic and political thought during the 1980s.

A second strain of the not-so-hidden agenda is represented by those in what can be described as the Provincial Rights Crowd. The Provincial Rights Crowd operates under a number of guises. There are the True Fiscal Conservatives, located principally in Ontario and Alberta, who believe that all state intervention and activity is bad: ours, yours, theirs. These folks don't want to promote things like daycare or social housing, and they don't want the feds or the municipalities promoting them either. At least give them points for consistency.

Then there is the Just Gimme the Money Bunch. Paradoxically, these people also include the True Fiscal Conservatives, who with one breath want to diminish the role of all government and reduce taxes for provincial taxpayers, and with the next want the federal government to ship large sums of money, no questions asked or conditions given, to provincial capitals forthwith. No thought here that federal taxpayers might actually deserve a break too, or that the federal debt should be paid down, and certainly no thought that there might be any new economic or social initiatives worth funding at the national level. Points off for inconsistency.

Provincial governments just want the funding restored to core social programs, not an unreasonable request, except they do not want to be held accountable for how the money is spent, nor do they want the federal government to monitor these programs to see if they are actually meeting their objectives. Just send the money, and on no account use your spending power to begin any new programs, however needed, however innovative, even if they are the initiative of one or two provinces, unless at least seven provinces agree beforehand, a condition roughly equivalent to and as imminent as the Second Coming.

A further complicating factor is that the federal government and the provinces agreed to conduct a series of negotiations aimed at renewing the social union. This was to be an overarching set of principles to which all other negotiations on social policy would be subordinated. All of this seemed perfectly sensible on paper. But the reality proved otherwise. Because most of the intergovernmental affairs ministers negotiating the renewal of the social union were not ministers with direct responsibility for social policy, any grievances (over the federal government's handling of the hepatitis-C file or the Millennium Scholarship Fund, for example) or good old-fashioned power struggles (over money or over which level of government should carry out some social program) forced social policy to take a back seat to the antics of the Masters of Outrage. And because intergovernmental affairs ministers are not paid to solve social problems but simply to advance the power interests of their governments, the royal road to headlines and glory lies in grievance and conflict.

As if the provincial rights issue wasn't thorny enough, in comes Quebec, that stormy petrel of provincial rights par excellence. The combination of reduced federal spending through deficit-cutting and program review and reduced federal self-confidence because of the narrow federalist victory in the 1995 Quebec referendum put Quebec in an excellent position to reassert its traditional demands for more power and autonomy. Meanwhile, the provinces, in their laudable eagerness to involve Quebec at any price in the negotiations to renew the social union, are playing a dangerous game, one that plays directly into the hands of Quebec separatists. It is all too easy for the provinces to ride on the Quebec tiger in demanding more power from the federal government, as if it were possible to get off the tiger at a comfortable distance from its final destination — Quebec's complete separation from Canada.

Quebec insists, as do many of the other provinces, that it is the exclusive role of the provinces to deliver social services, and that Ottawa's role is limited to providing financial support for those services. And Quebec carries the point even further, objecting to Canada's having any direct financial relationship with Quebecers. Hence the initial fury over the federal government's decision to provide direct financial assistance to post-secondary students through the Millennium Scholarship Fund, rather than funnelling the money through the governments of Quebec and the other provinces.

Quebec protests any federal intrusion in social policy, insisting that the provinces have the right to opt out of any national program with total compensation and virtually no restrictions placed on how they use the money instead. No wonder the other provinces are so anxious to have Quebec in their corner.

Faced with such a thicket of obstacles, and fearful of offending Quebec, the federal government has taken an understandably cautious approach to National Projects, both before and after the most recent Quebec election. It's better by far, the theory goes, to maintain a low profile and avoid creating any targets for Bouchard before the next referendum.

The only problem with this seemingly sensible approach is the dismal track record it has had thus far in Quebec. Caution and prudence were the watchwords of the federalist campaign in the 1995 Quebec referendum, and this strategy almost proved fatal in the face of the so-called Bouchard Effect. We are, thankfully, no further behind after the 1998 Quebec election, but we're no further ahead either. Surely it's better, then, for federalists to set an active positive agenda than to leave all sense of boldness, risk-taking, innovation, and national adventure in the hands of Lucien Bouchard.

Despite all these challenges, the current federal government has committed itself to increasing its investments in early childhood development. In terms of income support, the government has already pledged $1.7 billion to the new National Child Benefit, a program aimed at supporting the children of the working poor. And the Liberals made other commitments in their 1997 election platform (Red Book Two).

Red Book Two began by acknowledging the importance of early childhood intervention. "Research has proven consistently that investing in early support for families and children at risk yields real results. Community-based services play a critical role in helping parents ensure the healthy development of their children. By helping young children get off to a good start and preventing problems before they occur, these programs significantly reduce the need for far greater spending in the future." The policy book then spoke of the need to work in partnership: "These problems are complex, however, and will not be solved overnight. They require a concerted effort by federal and provincial governments alike, with the cooperation and support of the private and voluntary sectors and individual Canadians."

The Liberals pledged that their government would work with the provinces and territories to develop a National Children's Agenda, "a collective strategy to improve the well-being of Canada's children. The federal government welcomes this opportunity to develop a broader, more comprehensive framework for federal, provincial, and territorial initiatives. Given the strength of the current consensus on children's issues, there is every reason to believe that together we can establish clear national objectives for Canada's children, as well as a plan to achieve them. A new Liberal government is committed to working in partnership with Canada's provincial and territorial governments to develop a National Children's Agenda."

The Red Book said that a crucial element of the strategy was "that we set tangible objectives and benchmarks for the future, and measure our progress accordingly." Therefore, "a new Liberal government will undertake to measure and report, on a regular basis, the readiness to learn of Canadian children as they enter school. These results will help guide our policy and investment decisions concerning children and make them more effective." The Liberals also committed themselves to spending more money on the Community Action Program for Children and the Canada Prenatal Nutrition Program.

After the June 1997 election, the Speech from the Throne reiterated these promises:

A country that has decided to invest in its children is a country that is confident in its future. A country that invests in its children successfully will have a better future. One of our objectives as a country should be to ensure that all Canadian children have the best possible opportunity to develop their full potential. We must equip our children with the capacities they need to be ready to learn and to participate fully in our society.

While families have the greatest responsibility in the nurturing and development of our children, they are not alone. Developing our children requires a concerted effort and partnership by parents, governments, and the private and voluntary sectors. It requires focusing on what children need to thrive.

The experiences of Canada's children, especially in the early years, influence their health, their well-being, and their ability to learn and adapt throughout their entire lives. By investing now in the well-being of today's children, we improve the long-term health of our society. Addressing the needs of low-income families with children is therefore a priority of the government.

Amen.

ARE THERE PROVINCIAL ALLIES FOR A NATIONAL PROJECT FOR CHILDREN?

Should it decide to launch such a National Project, the federal government would not have to go it alone. In January 1997, at a meeting of the Ministerial Council on Social Policy Renewal, the federal, provincial, and territorial governments agreed to work together to develop a National Children's Agenda, a collective strategy to improve the well-being of Canada's children. Discussions surrounding the National Children's Agenda have been carried out by those federal and provincial ministers with specific responsibilities for children. Thus the federal representatives are the minister of Human Resources Development and the minister of Health. To outside observers, the talks have been maddeningly short on specifics, but there have also been several positive aspects to the process.

First, it is good news that the talks are happening at all, given the acrimony surrounding federal-provincial relations in other fields. True, the National Children's Agenda has periodically been superseded by other issues, most notably the discordant negotiations on the social union. But many of the civil servants involved, both federally and provincially, have a high degree of personal commitment to the process, and this commitment is shared by a number of their political superiors.

Second, the National Children's Agenda continues to command a high degree of provincial support, at least verbally. At their annual meeting in August 1997 in New Brunswick, the premiers publicly declared the National Children's Agenda to be a top priority. The final communiqué of a meeting between the premiers and the prime minister in Ottawa in December 1997 reiterated the commitment of all first ministers to the agenda. And after the premiers' annual gathering in Saskatoon in August 1998, they issued this encouraging press release on the National Children's Agenda:

Premiers acknowledged recent expressions of broad public support for a new national initiative and cooperative approaches to enhance the well-being of Canadian children, and reaffirmed their strong commitment to "fast-track" work on the National Children's Agenda. . . . Premiers endorsed the work of the Council on Social Policy Renewal to strengthen public involvement through the development of a shared vision for the Children's Agenda. They encouraged the Council to finalize its discussion paper and develop options for engaging the public in developing a shared vision for enhancing the well-being of Canada's children.

Third, among those most intimately involved in the discussions, there is a clear understanding of both the human development theory that must support policy and the necessity for both levels of government to work together and with other partners. As well, the element of public education and involvement has been properly stressed in the background documents. A National Project for Canada's Children, if it were properly carried out, would not only represent a fundamentally different way of conducting social policy in Canada, but also create a fundamentally new way of thinking about early childhood in its social context. It would be the equivalent of the revolution in educational theory that occurred in Western societies in the nineteenth century, when education ceased to be seen as a sporadic private activity for the children of the privileged and became a state funded, state-administered right for all children.

The National Children's Agenda, then, is a promising vehicle, a potentially useful process, an empty vessel into which meaning, policies, and programs can be poured. Such is the level of official commitment that the National Children's Agenda offers Canadians the opportunity to call the bluff of their provincial and federal politicians.

Moreover, individual provinces have already begun to institute policies that are entirely consistent with such a National Project. Paradoxically, given its objections to federal intrusion in this and all other areas of social policy, Quebec is leading Canada with its enlightened policy on early childhood development. Quebec's commitment to children predates the election of the Parti Québécois in 1994. It is truly a societal commitment, bigger than any one political party, and therefore is likely to survive the rise or fall of any specific party or government.

A good example of Quebec's commitment to its children can be found in the daycare system. Modelled on the *maternelle* system in France, it is the most complete publicly funded daycare program in Canada. After the most recent reforms, the poorest Quebec citizen will be able to send his or her child to daycare for five dollars a day, a rate that residents of other provinces can only dream of.

It is Quebec's very strength in the field of early childhood care and education that should encourage the rest of Canada to create a National Project. Just as Saskatchewan was the model for public health insurance in the 1960s, so too should Quebec be the model for early childhood development. We should be saying to Quebecers that we want to work with them to strengthen and support their programs in this area, that we want to use them as inspiration for the rest of Canada. It is difficult to imagine how such a discerning, warm, and admiring embrace could be turned against us. Indeed, such a strategy might have positive implications for national unity, showing, as it would, the strength in the diversity of our federation, which allows individual jurisdictions to undertake social experiments that might benefit the whole country. Such leadership should engender a well-deserved sense of pride in Quebec and respect in the rest of Canada.

But although it is the most advanced province, Quebec is far from alone in its innovative approach to child policy. Provinces like British Columbia, Nova Scotia, and even Ontario have begun the difficult process of integrating the diverse departments that deal with children (a task that puts them well ahead of the federal government in this regard). Saskatchewan several years ago created the Saskatchewan Action Plan for Children, which it continues to pursue actively. Prince Edward Island has created Child Alliance, a creative blend of private and public institutions designed to produce a comprehensive policy for early childhood development on the island.

Properly viewed, then, the provinces are not only an essential component of any National Project for children, they can also be valuable leaders, allies, and advocates. The challenge will be to rally them to the cause in a manner that they will find collaborative and respectful. Not an easy task, but not an impossible one either.

COMMUNITY INITIATIVES: THE REAL ASSETS FOR A NATIONAL PROJECT

Any successful National Project must be built, in part, on existing assets and initiatives. Fortunately, there is already a groundswell of experimentation and innovation taking place in communities across Canada in the field of early childhood care and education. Somehow, this energy must be harnessed to power our National Project.

In Montreal, an initiative called 1, 2, 3, Go! has been working in six communities with parents, local institutions, and citizens to help young children reach their potential through a variety of endeavours, including reading programs, parenting workshops, improved daycare centres and drop-in centres, and work on housing and nutrition problems. Most important, however, the community as a whole has mobilized around these issues. Collectively, a culture is being created to support early childhood development at the civic, and not simply individual, level.

Meanwhile, Vancouver is developing a project that focuses on children from conception to age six, and that uses school-readiness indicators to measure its results. The project's impressive array of partners includes the Vancouver school board, the health board, the social planning department, the City of Vancouver itself, the police department, the library system, the Department of Parks and Recreation, and at the provincial level, the new Ministry for Children and Families, the B.C. Council for the Family, and a broad coalition of community agencies. All are dedicated to establishing a community-based hub of services across the city, particularly (but not exclusively) in areas with a high number of families and children at risk.

The Vancouver model has three main components: family resource centres, a whole range of child care services, and a home visitation program. Lois Yelland, a public health doctor and leader in developing the proposal, believes Vancouver has a model that has national significance, and could be used across the country, because it involves all levels of government partnering with the city. "We believe this will pay big dividends in the long run. It's not a short-term investment; it's a long-term investment, and a significant one in terms of the funds we're asking for. But it has all kinds of implications in health, in justice, in social services, and in education, with savings down the road, not to mention the enormous savings in human terms."

What Vancouver would like to achieve, the former City of North York is well on its way to realizing through its Early Years Action Group, which began in 1996 as a coalition of government institutions, social agencies, and community groups. The mission was to mobilize existing resources around a unified vision of what the chief organizers believed about children, using two key benchmarks: birth weight and school readiness. Clara Will, who was instrumental in launching the initiative, speaks of the philosophy of the group:

> The main part of our thrust is to mobilize local neighbourhoods to plan for their own children, because the neighbourhoods know their children best. . . . Our plan is to look at what the needs of children are at each developmental stage and plan what conditions and situations are needed in order for those kids to have the best chance. We'll also make sure there's an infrastructure supporting the local neighbourhoods and advocate for economic policies that support the infrastructure. . . . We believe the parents or guardians have the main responsibility for raising their children, but they cannot do it alone. Today especially, they cannot do it alone, as many people are living in isolation and with all the stresses they have.

These are but three examples, taken from across the country, of the literally hundreds of community initiatives with similar goals. Their strength is in their numbers; their weakness is in their isolation from each other. A National Project could draw these ventures together, partner them with all levels of government, and encourage collaboration and the dissemination of information across the country. Such a binding together would find willing and ready allies in an astonishing variety of national and provincial organizations that have already committed themselves to improving early childhood development and school readiness. A few examples:

- A number of United Ways across Canada have banded together to promote their version of school readiness, the Success by Six Program.
- The Canadian School Boards Association has issued a challenge to all governments to focus investment on preschool development.
- In partnership with the CBC, *Canadian Living* magazine, and several major private corporations, the Invest in Kids Foundation is mounting a major campaign, called Fit for Life, to promote early childhood development.
- The Canadian Child Care Federation, the Canadian Public Health Association, the Canadian Institute for Child Health, the National Council of Welfare, Campaign 2000, the Caledon Institute, and the Family Network of the Canadian Policy Research Networks all have existing resources that such a National Project could draw upon.

We also know that public opinion would support such an initiative. Ekos Consulting has continually polled Canadians about their support for National Projects in general and for a National Project on children in particular. The results should give comfort to even the most cautious politician.

When Ekos asked Canadians, in December 1996, how important they thought it was for the government to produce a list of National Projects that could serve as goals for Canadian society, 64 percent said "very important," 22 percent said "somewhat important," and only 13 percent said "not important." When these same Canadians were asked to rate the appeal of specific National Projects, 85 percent endorsed "ensuring support and nurturing to Canadian children in the early years of their lives," and 82 percent supported "an initiative to improve the health of infants and their mothers."

SO HOW DO WE DO IT?

We have a powerful and urgent need. We know what must be done. We have our mission statement. We have the commitment of all governments to the National Children's Agenda. We have some constitutional flexibility. We have some money and a great number of other assets. We have models. We have existing government programs to build upon. We have enthusiasm and excitement in communities across Canada. We have public support.

So what's missing? Most crucially, a sense of national vision and a focused commitment that can come only from leadership at the federal and provincial levels.

How can we persuade our national leaders to take a chance, to embark on this adventure? By setting out a plausible course of action that divides the tasks to be done into manageable chunks and sets them within manageable time frames and realistic budgets.

1. The Mission Statement

Let's begin by returning to the mission statement. A National Project for Canada's Children will ensure that every child in Canada is "ready to learn" at entrance to formal school education. Remember: this seemingly innocuous mission statement was chosen because "this condition requires that the primary needs common to all children, and the additional special needs of some, have been met from conception to six years. The child is then cognitively, emotionally, socially, and physically ready to learn according to individual potential."

2. Three Crucial Elements

Two of the three crucial elements of our National Project are contained in this paragraph. First, we need to gauge how we are doing with young children, and the best way of doing that is to measure the readiness to learn of all Canadian children when they enter kindergarten. Second, the National Project must be directed not only at poor children and children at risk, but at all children. Both of these concepts require elaboration before we move on to the third crucial element: community mobilization.

Readiness to Learn

What, exactly, is readiness to learn? It is an indicator that measures children's preparedness to learn as they enter school by looking at five areas: physical health and well-being; social competence; emotional maturity; language richness; and general knowledge and cognitive skills.

Why is it done at age six? Researcher Magdalena Janus of the Centre for Studies of Children at Risk, based in Hamilton, Ontario, explains: "By the time children are six years old, they have developed basic language and cognitive skills, forming the base from which they acquire reading, writing, mathematical and higher reasoning abilities. Research has also shown that children's social and emotional competence up to adulthood and beyond has its roots in prosocial and social behaviour at four to five years of age."

Why not measure this earlier? Because of obligatory school attendance, kindergarten is the first time since birth that it is possible to measure all children in a community. Birth weight is the only piece of universally collected data on children's well-being before school entry. While it would be useful to have a third measure in that period between birth and age six, which is referred to by some researchers as an informational "black hole," there is, at present, no easy way of collecting such data either locally or nationally.

Who does the measuring and how? It takes a trained kindergarten teacher between ten and twenty minutes to complete the readiness-to-learn indicator for each child. The teacher provides scores for each of the five areas, as well as a total score.

Does it discriminate against or stigmatize individual students? Dr. Janus says, "The instrument is not designed to provide data at the individual level, because it is designed to work at the group level and thus is not sensitive enough to be used to assess individual children. Individual children are not identified, and the results of the score are not stored in the child's records. The test concludes with a question about the necessity of a further assessment of the child's needs, and the teacher's answer to that question may be used as a guide to provide help for individual children in the school context."

So what does the readiness-to-learn measure tell us about groups of students? First, it provides a snapshot of the weaknesses and strengths of a group of students in a specific community. Second, it assesses the effectiveness of early childhood interventions in that community. Finally, it predicts how those children will do in elementary school.

If the damage has been done by the time a child is six, what good will measurements taken after the fact be for that specific child? First, for the class and school where the children are being tested, the readiness indicator can identify developmental gaps. Armed with this knowledge, teachers can try to alter the trajectory and improve the future lives of those children. For individual children, as shown, the readiness test may indicate the need for further review, which in turn may allow teachers to deal with specific problems at the earliest possible moment. Second, measuring readiness to learn at school entry allows for a far fairer later assessment of how teachers and schools are doing than an arbitrary and universal test in Grade Three, which is now being used in Ontario.

All Children

Earlier we indicated that a second crucial element of any successful National Project was that it had to address the interests of *all* Canadian children. Why? The easier and more obvious course of action is to focus on poor children and children at risk, which is where the childhood developmental problems and needs are greatest. But while it is true that the special needs of some children will inevitably require more resources than the general needs of all, there are three compelling reasons for a National Project to be inclusive rather than exclusive.

First, no Canadian child, even one born into the greatest privilege, can thrive in total isolation from the rest of the community. All of us need help. Whether it is the first-time mother being visited by a public health nurse, new parents needing a parenting course, or an affluent two-income household with a desperate need for high-quality early childhood care and education; whether we need community drop-in programs and accessible recreation facilities; whether we simply want advice from a neighbourhood parent resource centre about programs available in the community — we all need help beyond the family circle.

We also want to know that the children our children will inevitably be meeting in the park, on the street, and in daycare are also thriving, because the quality of our children's earliest social interactions will be affected by the health and well-being of these other children. We want our children to have positive experiences when they socialize, because the quality of those experiences, over time, can make them either confident about or fearful of life. In other words, we all have a vested interest in improving the lot of every child, either because we want a positive environment within which our own children may flourish or because we simply want to live in a safer, healthier, better-educated, friendlier community.

A second reason for including all Canadian children in our National Project is that we are trying to effect a societal change. We are trying to reorient society's traditional view that the care and nurturing of young children is essentially a private matter, and hence an essentially chaotic, happenstance event, whose outcome is determined by the luck of the draw. This is the way we used to think about education in the nineteenth century, and it is the way Americans still think about health care in the late twentieth century. If our National Project is to change the paradigm, we will have to begin to think about early childhood development the way we now think about public education and public health care. This is a revolution in thinking that can come about only if we see all of our children, and hence all of us, being involved.

The final reason for taking an inclusive approach is purely (or impurely) political. If we are to have solid, broad public support, we need to show all Canadians that there is something in it for them and their families, that they personally will be better off if we can improve life for all Canadian children. The moment we focus our efforts exclusively on poor or at-risk children, we lose support, particularly among those taxpayers who already feel overburdened and just want a tax cut.

Community Mobilization

If we wish to improve the well-being of all young children in Canada, we can do so only at the community level. Actual geographic communities create the physical and social environments in which children and families live. If we are to improve those environments, we need some method for rallying the community. Herein lies the real importance of promoting the use of the readiness-to-learn measure at the community level.

The measure gives communities the power to improve the quality of local early childhood development. Readiness to learn is a "mobilizing benchmark," which means that it can be used to prompt corrective action, with the aim of raising the community's score for the betterment of all its children. Measuring school readiness allows a community to reach back into the pre-existing network of support to identify gaps, assess the quality of institutions (publicly funded, not-for-profit daycare versus private, unregulated daycare, for example), and make changes that will result in better community-wide readiness scores.

In other words, those who can learn the most from school-readiness scores are not academic researchers, curious statisticians, or policy wonks, but the communities themselves. For a National Project on children to work, communities have to mobilize, assess the specific development needs of all children under age six by using school-readiness indicators, then take whatever collective action is needed with all the other partners we've mentioned. But neither a National Project nor school-readiness tests can be foisted on an unwilling community. Communities must actively want to improve the lives of their young children, and must want to do so in an informed manner that can result only from wide and serious consultation beforehand.

The most that governments, particularly the federal government, can do initially is to offer to provide the tools a community needs to call the meeting, to disseminate the latest knowledge on early childhood development, to conduct an informed discussion and consultation, to self-assess, to mobilize, to measure progress and outcomes, and to expedite communication with other like-minded communities so that best practices and common problems may be easily shared. Then, using the framework of the National Children's Agenda, the federal government would have both the information and the public support it would need to recruit other governments and private sector partners into filling the gaps such an exercise would reveal.

Community mobilization, then, is the third component that needs to be in place for the successful implementation of a National Project on children.

3. First Steps

Given the breadth of our ambitions, it may seem paradoxical for us to suggest that the first step is for all of us to agree that, for the moment, we will create no new programs. Instead, we will simply work with the old ones, modifying and amplifying them as necessary.

Why? The first reason is political necessity. As long as the provinces continue to insist, rightly or wrongly, that there must be no new programs until we have restored funding to the old ones, we must accept this as a pre-condition for what we propose.

Also, a number of programs, both federal and provincial, are either just coming on stream, as is the case with the National Child Benefit, or have reached a stage where evaluation and reconfiguring is appropriate, as is the case with the federal government's Community Action Program for Children (CAPC). We need to take the time to lay out all our existing and emerging assets to see how they can be made to fit together before we launch anything new. We also need to involve Canadians in our discussions through the mechanisms proposed by the premiers, using the National Children's Agenda and the Council on Social Policy Renewal, however imperfect these instruments may be.

The National Children's Agenda offers us the framework within which to move forward. For us to initiate a National Project for children under the age of six, we must start by declaring that such a project would be only a first step, since the National Children's Agenda has, as its focus, children from conception to the age of eighteen. It divides its analysis into four "transition periods": transition to life (conception to eighteen months); transition to school (eighteen months to five years); transition to adolescence (six to twelve years); and transition to adulthood (thirteen to eighteen years). Given this, we believe that the National Project we propose has two virtues: it begins at the beginning, by getting the foundations for human development right; and it encompasses two of the four transition periods outlined by the National Children's Agenda.

So which existing programs and resources could be usefully deployed to help us meet our three immediate objectives of readiness to learn, community mobilization, and some degree of universality? And how can we realign these existing programs to ensure that each stage of human development is supported by adequate resources within each community?

Logically, we need to begin with community mobilization. It is true that the readiness-to-learn indicator is a powerful tool for community mobilization, but the community really needs to mobilize first to discuss whether it even wants to try implementing such a measure in its schools, let alone how and when it might do so.

Fortunately, when it comes to community mobilization, we are not starting with a blank canvas. As we've indicated, many communities are already mobilized; they just need better access to resources and improved communication with other communities. As well, a number of existing programs and organizations have already had some experience with community mobilization. We simply need to learn which models have been most successful, and build on those to improve existing efforts while inspiring and expediting new ones. Two examples will suffice: the Community Action Program for Children (CAPC) and the Success by Six Program of the United Way of Canada.

In 1993, in response to pledges made during the International Year of the Child, the Mulroney government negotiated a series of twelve bilateral agreements with the provinces and territories to create the Community Action Program for Children. The primary targets were at-risk children from conception to age six. The philosophy underlying the program was entirely consistent with the human development theory discussed above. The approach was to be community-based and holistic, with communities uniting to pull existing resources together while identifying and filling gaps. Although it recognized the primacy of the provincial role in providing social services, the federal government worked cooperatively with the provinces and with communities to strengthen and improve the network of resources available to families with young children. CAPC agreements also provided for ongoing evaluations of specific programs.

There are now 450 CAPC programs in communities in every province and territory, including Quebec. The programs have been a hit with all provinces and many communities. And most important, two major goals have been achieved. First, a number of successful models for community mobilization have been uncovered; these include models for conditions ranging from small towns to multicultural cities to aboriginal communities. Thus the experience of the CAPC program can be used to help other communities mobilize.

Second, in existing CAPC communities an institutional base has been created, and that base can be built upon and new partners can be added. Prince Edward Island's six CAPC programs, for example, effectively cover the island's main administrative areas, and it is one of these CAPCs — CHANCES in Charlottetown — that is spearheading Child Alliance (mentioned earlier in this chapter).

CAPC, then, gives us an institutional base from which to begin to build a National Project. It requires no new agreements with the provinces. It can be expanded upon and improved on the basis of the last five years' experience. Since the federal government is responsible for the periodic evaluation of all programs, and there is nothing in the agreements that precludes the use of readiness to learn as one of the evaluation mechanisms, why should we not apply a such a measure? Thus CAPC is an existing program that could help us move towards achieving two of our goals: community mobilization and promoting readiness to learn.

But CAPC doesn't have to do it all. The United Way of Canada/Centraide Canada has 125 local chapters in communities across the country, and covers 90 percent of Canadians. It is the single largest non-government funder of voluntary sector health and social services for all Canadians, including children. The United Way is looking at developing a framework for network-wide adoption and implementation of Success by Six programs. Since the United Way/Centraide Canada has an unblemished reputation for providing high-quality services, forging partnerships, building community potential, taking an integrated approach to human development, and emphasizing preventative measures, it could play a key role in a National Project, both in mobilizing communities and in expanding the reach of services offered to all Canadian children.

We don't lack resources for our National Project, we lack willpower and coordination. With the National Children's Agenda, the federal government, should it wish to make Canada's children a priority, has a useful instrument for calling the initial meeting with the provinces and all other interested parties. It has the existing programs. It has the tax structure. And as Canada's national government, it surely has the right to talk directly to Canadians and deal directly with the communities in which they live.

In short, what it will take to achieve this National Project is vision, willpower, and leadership. Stay tuned.

8

A National Project on New Energy Systems

For the past couple of years, a strange-looking transit bus has been roaming the streets of Vancouver, pilot-testing the energy technology that will dominate the twenty-first century. What makes the bus look unusual are the hydrogen fuel tanks on the roof towards the back of the vehicle. The bus is powered by fuel cells developed by Ballard Power Systems, a Canadian company that is one of the leading international contenders in the race to what is becoming known as the hydrogen economy.

Ballard's fuel cells represent a revolutionary new technology. Through an electro-chemical reaction, they convert hydrogen and oxygen into electrical power. The by-products of this process are heat and a small quantity of water vapour — pure H_2O. Unlike internal or external combustion engines, hydrogen fuel cells emit no greenhouse gases, carbon monoxide, or other pollutants. For a world facing the nightmare of potentially irreversible damage to the earth's ecosystem as a result of excessive greenhouse gas emissions, accelerating deforestation, destruction of ocean habitat, nuclear waste, and upper-atmosphere ozone depletion, hydrogen fuel cells seem like a dream come true.

Ballard isn't the only company developing fuel cells, but it is clearly the farthest ahead on the road to full commercialization. Ballard's technology has attracted interest from major automobile companies, manufacturers of power-generation equipment, electrical utilities, stock market investors, and governments because it has the potential to solve many of the problems that have constrained the widespread adoption of other alternative energy technologies based on solar or wind power. It is easily scaleable — that is, fuel cells can be built small enough to power a portable computer or large enough to power a medium-sized city. One of the principal problems with solar or wind power is the storing of the power between the time it is generated and the time it is needed. Fuel cells solve that problem by not generating power until it is needed. Perhaps most important, from a short-term perspective, fuel cells can be modified to operate using existing fuel sources such as natural gas and even gasoline.

Compared with the technologies they are destined to replace, however, fuel cells are still in their infancy, and face many technical and cost hurdles before widespread adoption is feasible. Internal combustion engines have been perfected by more than a century of development (the theory underlying the internal combustion engine was first published in 1862, and working engines emerged in the late 1860s and early 1870s). The basic technologies supporting electricity generation and transmission were developed in the late 1800s, and were implemented throughout the twentieth century in successive waves of dam-building and grid development, followed by a proliferation of oil-burning and, eventually, nuclear power plants.

Despite these challenges, however, many are predicting that as the twenty-first century proceeds, we will see a gradually accelerating shift to hydrogen and similar "clean" fuels for heat, electricity generation, and transportation. The argument goes that in the 1700s and all previous centuries, the main energy source (apart from the sun and domestic animals) was wood. During the 1800s, the main energy source for heating, transportation, and industrial production was coal, although energy from water was used where possible to power grain, saw, and textile mills. In the twentieth century, oil (and in the last couple of decades, various hydrocarbon-based gases) replaced coal as the dominant energy source for heating, transportation, and electrical generation. In each of the last two centuries, we have seen a continuing shift towards more concentrated, cleaner forms of energy than we've seen in the previous century. According to this theory, hydrogen is the logical next step.

Given these developments, Canada has two choices. It could choose to be a laggard in the development and implementation of the energy technologies that will dominate the twenty-first century. Or we could collectively decide to be a leader in accelerating our transition to new energy systems and, in the process, generate export revenues by helping other countries make the transition to cleaner forms of energy.

We support the latter alternative. We believe that Canadians should create a National Project on New Energy Systems.

WHY THE STATUS QUO IS NOT AN OPTION

In two words: climate change. During the 1990s, scientific opinion gradually shifted to the view that there was finally enough evidence to conclude that human activity was affecting the global climate. While there are many factors that contribute to climate change, the main problem is greenhouse gases — water vapour, carbon dioxide, methane, and nitrous oxide — which trap heat inside the earth's atmosphere. The concern is that the burning of fossil fuels, combined with deforestation, is increasing greenhouse gases to the point that average temperatures are rising. This could have significant destabilizing impacts throughout the planet, leading to higher sea levels, disruption of agricultural production, and irreversible damage to global ecosystems.

Faced with the scientific evidence, the international community gradually came to the conclusion that some action was needed to limit greenhouse gas emissions, and launched a process of international negotiations. In December 1997, Canada and 160 other countries met in Kyoto, Japan, to ratify a protocol that called for each nation to manage its greenhouse gas emissions over the following fifteen years.

In Canada's case, the Kyoto Protocol calls for emissions to be 6 percent lower than 1990 levels by the year 2012. This might not sound like much, but it is an enormous challenge. In 1990, it was estimated that Canada's carbon dioxide (or CO_2 equivalent) emissions were 599 megatons. Canada's target under the Kyoto Protocol is 563 megatons. By 1997, however, Canada's emissions had jumped to more than 670 megatons, and were projected to be between 700 and 750 megatons by 2012 if no action was taken. Effectively, then, Canada must achieve a reduction of 20 to 25 percent.

An impressive process has been launched to help Canada accomplish this goal. Federal and provincial energy and environment ministers met in April 1998 to design the National Climate Change Process, with the objective of developing a national implementation strategy by the end of 1999. This process is being coordinated by a National Climate Change Secretariat, which includes representatives of the federal and provincial governments. Fifteen "issue tables" have been set up to carry out the analysis needed to develop a plan covering all sectors of Canada's economy and society. A website has been set up to communicate progress at http://www.nccp.ca.

Even if this process fully achieves its goals, however, it may not be enough. Many argue that Canada's Kyoto commitment was not sufficiently aggressive — that continuing to release 563 megatons of CO_2 into the atmosphere is unacceptable in view of the risks of global climate change. Environmentalists point out that industrialized countries like Canada have been the main contributors to greenhouse gases in the past, and therefore have a moral obligation to make far greater reductions to leave room for developing countries to increase their energy use as they industrialize.

In the long run, the greenhouse gas problem is tied to how we generate the energy needed for transportation, heating, lighting, running factories, and so on. Today, approximately 75 percent of Canada's total energy use involves burning fossil fuels — natural gas, oil, and coal, in that order. The balance comes mainly from hydroelectric and nuclear power generation. Ultimately, solving the greenhouse gas problem requires finding new ways to produce energy that don't burn fossil fuels in vehicles, furnaces, and power-generation plants. Since most of the accessible hydro sites in Canada are already exploited, and since there are profound problems associated with expanding nuclear power, we need to think in a fundamentally different way about energy systems.

NEW ENERGY SYSTEMS

This brings us back to Ballard Power Systems, and why so many people are excited about fuel cell technology. For the first time, there is a technology that generates energy efficiently with no greenhouse gas emissions, and that overcomes the limitations of traditional alternative energy technologies.

Solar and wind power have been around for centuries. However, they have major problems that have limited their adoption on a significant scale. With the exception of sailing, they are of no practical use in transportation — you can't mount a wind generator on your car. They could be used to charge the batteries in an electric vehicle, but the related costs have so far put this out of the reach of the average Canadian.

Anyone wishing to retrofit his or her home for solar or wind power faces a daunting task. Weeks of research are needed to find the right combination of equipment to fit the particular application. If you want to use heat from the sun to warm your home, you have to find a way to store that heat for periods when the sun is not shining. This means creating a large thermal mass in your home — typically either a giant water tank or a room full of rocks. Neither is appealing to most people.

If you decide you want to capture energy from the sun in the form of electricity, you will soon discover that while solar photovoltaic panels are readily available, you still face the problem of storing the electricity for the hours when the sun is not shining. This means a room full of lead-acid batteries, a controller to ensure that they don't get overcharged, a diversion device to use up the excess energy produced when there's more power available than your batteries can absorb, and an inverter to turn the power in your batteries into 120 volts so it can run your lights and appliances. This all costs many thousands of dollars, and most people can't justify the expense unless they're in a location that's remote from the power grid.

Wind-generated electricity has the same problems as photovoltaics. Apart from the wind generator, you need thousands of dollars' worth of other equipment to store energy for when the wind isn't blowing. There are a few places in Canada where wind generation is used on an industrial scale. In general, however, the cost of installing large wind or solar arrays is too large to justify, compared with the much lower costs of electricity from the local power utility.

Fuel cells, however, have the potential to change the equation. They allow us to envision electricity and transportation systems that are radically different from the ones we have now. In other words, they're not just an interesting technology that could be developed as a Strategic Opportunity, they are catalysts for systemic change. Let's start with electricity.

NEW ELECTRICITY SYSTEMS

Currently, electricity production is centralized in huge hydro, thermal, or nuclear generating stations, strategically located across the country. Electricity is distributed using a massive one-way power grid that transports it from the generating stations to the consumers. Since electricity can't be stored, the amount of electricity generated must continually be adjusted to match consumption throughout the grid. This requires a complex coordination process that links the provincial energy utilities with their counterparts in other provinces and U.S. states.

Fuel cells allow us to imagine a different kind of system. A 250 kilowatt fuel cell system capable of generating the power needed by a neighbourhood of fifty to sixty homes is about the size of a shipping container. Rather than centralized electricity generation, we could have a system where generation is more widely distributed. Rather than a one-way grid, we could have a two-way grid, which would enable one city to supply excess energy to a neighbouring city and vice versa. These possibilities are closer than you might think. In May 1998, Ballard announced a $110-million deal with ALSTOM, a $16-billion French company that manufactures power generation and transportation systems. Under the agreement, Ballard and ALSTOM will collaborate in the development and marketing of Ballard's initial stationary power plants, sized at 250 kilowatts, which are expected to be in service by 2001. GPU International, a New Jersey–based company, and the EBARA Corporation of Japan have also invested in Ballard's power generation technology.

But our imaginations can roam even further than this. A fuel cell capable of generating the power needed by the average household is about the size of a small refrigerator. A two-way grid would allow consumers to generate their own electricity, take additional power from the grid when necessary, and sell any excess power back to the grid. Honda and Matsushita Electric Works have already purchased fuel cell systems from Ballard that could be used in portable generators.

A logical question is, where would the hydrogen to run these fuel cells come from? One source is the hydrogen in natural gas. We could use the existing distribution network to supply gas to power both city-sized and consumer-sized fuel cells. Another option is to use electricity to extract hydrogen from water. Two Ontario-based companies, the Electrolyser Corporation and Stuart Energy Systems, are world leaders in technology that uses electricity to split water into its constituent components —

hydrogen and oxygen. But what's the point of using electricity to generate hydrogen, only to turn around and use the hydrogen to generate electricity, you might ask.

The answer is that the hydrogen becomes a way of storing electricity. It solves the problem, described above, of storing solar or wind power when the sun isn't shining or the wind isn't blowing, which currently requires a roomful of expensive lead-acid batteries. Cities or individuals could use solar or wind power to generate hydrogen, and then use the stored hydrogen to generate electricity as required.

Another potential source of hydrogen is hydroelectric power. Quebec and Labrador, for example, have considerable excess hydroelectric generation capacity, particularly in off-peak times. Rather than gearing down the turbines at night, which is currently the practice, these utilities could run them flat out all the time, and use the power not needed for immediate consumption to generate hydrogen.

Now we can begin to see the shape of a National Project on New Energy Systems as it relates to electricity generation and distribution. The long-term goal, which could be achieved late in the next century, would be to create an electrical generation system that produces no greenhouse gases. Accomplishing this would involve every part of Canada. British Columbia is the headquarters of Ballard Power. Alberta and Atlantic Canada could supply natural gas to power fuel cells in many parts of the country. Ontario is the headquarters of the Electrolyser Corporation and Stuart Energy Systems. Quebec, Newfoundland, and other provinces have excess hydroelectric capacity. The federal government has already been an important supporter of Ballard, and has a coordination role to play.

The process of gradually retro-fitting our existing electricity system to encourage the proliferation of fuel cells would create tremendous opportunities for every utility in the country, as well as for the private sector and private citizens. The possibilities are truly enormous.

NEW ENERGY SYSTEMS FOR TRANSPORTATION

The other major area of opportunity for the use of fuel cells is transportation. About a third of Canada's CO_2 emissions come from transportation. Of this, slightly over half result from passenger transportation, and the balance from freight.

Emissions are directly related to fuel consumption. In the 1970s, automotive and truck manufacturers were under intense pressure to increase fuel efficiency, which doubled between 1973 and 1983. However, since 1983, there has been no significant increase in overall fuel efficiency. This is partly because no jurisdictions, apart from the State of California, have put major pressure on the automakers. But there are also basic limits to the technology of the internal combustion engine. If we want to achieve a major reduction in emissions, we have to look at a different technology.

One option is to encourage people to use public transportation. On a Canada-wide basis, however, this has been a complete flop. As a percentage of total passenger-kilometres in Canada, public transit is stuck below 5 percent. Even if this percentage were to double, which is unlikely, it wouldn't make much difference to total emissions.

Electric-powered vehicles provide another obvious option. However, the continuing problem here has been the storage capacity of current battery technology. Lead-acid batteries are too bulky and heavy to use for vehicles with a range greater than about one hundred kilometres per charge. Other types of batteries are still prohibitively expensive. Automakers realized early on that most consumers would be unwilling to pay more for a car with less range and flexibility than they currently enjoy.

Fuel cells, on the other hand, offer a zero-emission technology that is not subject to the disadvantages of battery-powered electrical vehicles, and that is significantly more fuel efficient than current gasoline or diesel engines. The space needed to store a tank of hydrogen is roughly the same as the space needed for a tank of gas — or will be shortly. Best of all, with slight modifications, fuel cell systems can be designed to extract the hydrogen from fuels such as gasoline, methanol, natural gas, and propane (with any fuel other than hydrogen there are some emissions, but far less than those resulting from combustion). Therefore, fuel cells can run on the energy sources that are already readily available, although the long-term objective should be to retrofit the fuel distribution system to supply hydrogen.

This is why most of the major auto companies are interested in Ballard's technology. In 1997, DaimlerChrysler injected $450 million into Ballard, bought 20 percent of its shares, and formed an alliance to commercialize fuel cell systems in transportation applications. In April 1998, a follow-on $600-million investment brought Ford into the DaimlerChrysler alliance and gave it a 15 percent stake in Ballard. General Motors, Honda, Mazda, and Nissan are also testing Ballard's technology. If you've recently bought a car, your next vehicle could well be powered by fuel cells. The DaimlerChrysler/Ford/Ballard alliance wants to have fuel-cell-powered vehicles on the market by 2004.

With help from the B.C. and Canadian governments, Ballard is also testing fuel cells for urban transit applications. The bus platforms are supplied by New Flyer, the Winnipeg-based bus manufacturer, and are being pilot-tested by B.C. Transit and the Chicago transit authority.

A major shift towards hydrogen fuel cells by auto, truck, and bus manufacturers would have obvious implications for fuel suppliers. This is why it was highly significant that Shell International flew more than a dozen top executives to Buenos Aires in June 1998. The Twelfth World Hydrogen Energy Conference was occurring there at the time. Taking advantage of the presence of leading international experts, Shell staffers arranged a one-day briefing session to discuss how Shell could move into the hydrogen business. A month later, Shell made a major announcement as Europe's first hydrogen-powered fuel cell taxicab made its debut in London. Chris Fay, the chief executive of Shell UK, said the event "is not just about the launch of an exciting new vehicle which promises cheaper, more efficient and environmentally friendly travel. It's about broader issues — the future of transport, the quality of the air we breathe, and ultimately, about the quality of life both here in the capital and in all of our major towns and cities."

Fay indicated that Shell had established a Hydrogen Economy team to look at opportunities for hydrogen manufacturing, and that the company was cooperating with Zevco, the maker of the hydrogen-powered taxicab, and Ballard's alliance company with DaimlerChrysler and Ford. Said Fay:

We believe that hydrogen fuel-cell-powered cars are likely to make a major entrance into the vehicle market throughout Europe and the U.S. by 2005. In addition, we see potentially enormous opportunities opening up in the domestic fleet, bus and taxi market as government encourages cleaner alternatives to conventionally powered vehicles.

This trend poses a real challenge to a company like Shell to develop new products, new technologies, and to prepare and inform our customers for the changes that lie ahead. This isn't going to happen overnight, but substantial planning and technological progress has already been made. I can assure you, we are in this for the long haul.

Mobil, Arco, Exxon, and Texaco are also looking at supplying energy sources for fuel cells. So not only will we be able to buy a fuel cell car in 2004, there's a good chance we'll be able to get a fill-up, too.

We can now begin to see who would be the major players in a National Project on New Energy Systems as they relate to transportation. Such a project would clearly involve B.C., as the home of Ballard Power; Manitoba, as the home of New Flyer; and Ontario and Quebec, as the home of most of Canada's auto production. It would involve the private sector players in the auto, bus, truck, rail, and shipping industries. It would involve the oil and gas industry, and everyone connected to the fuel distribution network. Ultimately, it would involve all of us when we make our next vehicle purchase.

A NATIONAL PROJECT ON NEW ENERGY SYSTEMS

We suggested above that Canada has two options: to lag behind in the development and implementation of the energy technologies that will dominate the twenty-first century, or to take a global leadership role.

If we want to take a leadership role, we need to get a move on. We're already behind Iceland. This country of only 260,000 people is developing a plan to convert itself to a hydrogen economy within fifteen to twenty years, and has approached both Ballard and DaimlerChrysler for technical assistance. Some of the options Iceland is considering include manufacturing hydrogen for export, as well as outfitting the nation's automobiles, buses, trucks, and even its fishing fleet with fuel cells. Iceland's parliament has already passed legislation that removes road taxes for zero-emission vehicles.

So what should Canada do?

The first thing is to agree on a vision or a mission statement. For example, we could decide that by the year 2025, we want to transform Canada from one of the leading per capita consumers of traditional energy to the world leader in the generation and distribution of energy from new energy systems. In addition, we could agree that we want to be one of the top five exporters of technology, products, and know-how relating to new energy systems.

We suggest that the project focus on "new energy systems" rather than the "hydrogen economy" because hydrogen will never be the only source of energy. There will always be a role, albeit a smaller one, for conventional fuels. In addition, we should stay open to the possibility that other breakthrough technologies may emerge.

After agreeing on the vision, we would need to decide collectively on the strategies that would get us there. Here are some suggestions:

1. We need a broadly based national process for identifying and validating promising technologies that can meet Canada's energy needs while still enabling us to exceed our Kyoto commitments and provide

a competitive advantage to the Canadian economy through greater energy efficiency. Fuel cells will undoubtedly be one of these, but there are other technologies that should be looked at as well. When these technologies are being developed in Canada, we should ensure that the proper support structure exists to facilitate their commercialization.

2. We should develop a set of broad specifications that will describe the infrastructures we need in place by 2025 to support the generation and transmission of electricity from new energy systems, as well as the manufacture and distribution of new transportation fuels. With this knowledge, we could then develop a plan to ensure that all of the capital improvements made to our existing infrastructures are compatible with these future specifications. For example, all normal maintenance and development of the power grid done over the next twenty-five years should facilitate its ultimate transition to a two-way grid. Similarly, all future investment in facilities in the fuel distribution network should be made with hydrogen in mind.

3. We should be asking what we need to do to make sure that Canada becomes a leading manufacturer of products relating to new energy systems. For example, Ford and DaimlerChrysler intend to roll out fuel-cell-powered vehicles by 2004. What do we need to do to make sure that the vehicles for the North American market are manufactured in Canada, and that Canada becomes the leading supplier of automotive fuel cells to the world? How can we make sure that Canadian parts manufacturers have a chance at the components contracts? What do we need to do to make sure that New Flyer becomes the leading integrator of fuel cell technologies into buses in North America, and a challenger for other world markets as well? What do we need to do to make sure that Canadian refineries are leaders in the production of the fuels of the new century? What do we need to do to make sure that Canada becomes a leading exporter of electrolyser technology? How do we get utilities across the country to take a positive approach to technologies relating to the new energy systems? How do we make

sure that Ballard becomes a world-class manufacturer and remains a Canadian company? (It would be tragic if, to finance its development, Ballard was forced to submit to a foreign takeover.)

In addressing these questions, we should also ensure that adequate capital is available to support the necessary investments. It may be appropriate to learn from Quebec's example, and use the pool of capital created by the new Canada Pension Plan funding mechanism as a means of supporting a leading role for Canada's private sector in new energy systems.

4. One of the key ways to influence the development of a global industry is to control the standards. Just ask Microsoft. By taking the initiative, we have the opportunity to lead the process of standards development for all aspects of new energy systems, and thereby create a competitive advantage for Canadian products. This is an area where government and private sector joint effort is essential.

5. We should examine ways to create incentives for early adopters of technologies relating to new energy systems. In the case of transportation products, this could include incentives for individuals, as well as for cab companies, delivery services, transit authorities, the military, and so on. In particular, federal, provincial, and municipal authorities should recognize the strategic importance of using procurement to create an early market for products relating to new energy systems. The influence of public sector institutions such as schools, universities, and hospitals should also be considered.

6. It is important to ensure that students and citizens are made aware of the strategic importance of new energy systems for Canada and the world, and that they develop the understanding and skills needed to feel comfortable acquiring and using these new technologies in their own lives. This has implications for school curricula, lifelong learning, and consumer education.

7. Taking a leaf from California's book, Canadian governments should put in place a regulatory regime that is compatible with new energy systems.

8. New energy systems will do a lot for Canadian cities. Anyone who has visited the mega-cities of developing countries knows that air pollution is a major problem that threatens the health of the population generally, and children particularly. It should be a Canadian priority to assist developing countries around the world in acquiring new technologies. The energy policies of India and China will ultimately have a far greater influence on global CO_2 emissions, and hence on climate change, than anything Canada does.

GETTING STARTED

The government of British Columbia and the federal government have already collaborated with Ballard in financing several key projects. This is a good place to start. We said earlier that not all National Projects need to be led by the federal government. In this case, why not ask B.C. to take the overall lead, with the offer of strong and enthusiastic support, and dollars, from the federal government? There are likely to be two major thrusts to this project — one focused on electrical generation and distribution, and the other on transportation. Perhaps Quebec should take the lead on the former and Ontario on the latter. But we shouldn't forget that virtually all provinces have a strategic interest in this initiative. Prime Minister Chrétien should ensure that the project is placed on the agenda of a First Ministers Conference at the earliest opportunity.

It is essential that the National Project on new energy systems be coordinated with the existing National Climate Change Process. Perhaps it should be managed through the same, or a related, secretariat. The key is to make sure that each of the two projects moves in parallel, with neither being held back by the other. One good reason to run the National Project in conjunction with the National Climate Change Process is that there is a risk that many in the private sector will perceive the effort to reduce emissions as one that will result only in higher costs and lower profits. By contrast, the National Project on new energy systems offers enormous wealth-creation opportunities to the private sector, in both Canadian and world markets.

Clearly, there must be strong leadership from the private sector, from Ballard, Electrolyser, Stuart Energy Systems, the oil and gas industry, the automotive manufacturing sectors, other transportation equipment manufacturers, and so on. All electrical utilities across the country should also be involved.

There is a major role for those in the Canadian research community as well. They can assist in doing the scientific, engineering, economic, and financial analyses needed to assess various strategic options and their implications, as well as help to solve some of the remaining technological challenges and enable early commercialization efforts.

ENVOI

This opportunity is one of those once-in-a-lifetime things. It's like Bill Gates when IBM came knocking on his door looking for an operating system. In this case, the world is already knocking on Ballard's door. Let's seize the day.

9

A National Project
on Educational New Media

In Chapter 3, we said that the most important event in Canada's cultural history, prior to the Internet, was the 1951 report of the Massey-Lévesque Commission. The most important event in Canada's cultural history since the Internet is SchoolNet. At one level, SchoolNet (http://www.schoolnet.ca) is a collection of Internet resources designed for students and teachers. At another level, SchoolNet represents the future of Canada's cultural policy.

To understand the importance of SchoolNet, we need to recognize that the legacy of the Massey-Lévesque Commission, and Canada's cultural policy of the last half century, is under fundamental attack. Technology and trade rules are combining to undermine the ability and the right of the federal government to maintain Canadian content regulations.

In 1997, the U.S. magazine industry won an important victory in its efforts to capture the 20 percent of Canadian shelf space and 11 percent of Canadian newsstand magazine sales that foreign magazines don't already own. The U.S. entertainment industry, supported by the U.S.

government, continues to be unsatisfied with anything less than complete and unrestricted access to the Canadian market, and regards the federal government's Canadian-content policies as pure protectionism. The Americans object to our regulations on content not only because they prevent U.S. industries from increasing their profits in Canada, but also because they act as an important symbol to all other nations that are concerned about the U.S. domination of mass media. If the Americans can successfully undermine Canada's content regulations using global trade laws, then they will have the ability to attack the cultural policy of France and other countries.

While the Canada-U.S. Free Trade Agreement and NAFTA upheld Canada's right to protect its cultural industries, the U.S. recently managed to find another route to attack Canadian content restrictions: the newly established World Trade Organization (WTO). In June 1997, a WTO ruling struck down the Canadian policies that restricted U.S. magazines from selling split-run editions in Canada. For American magazines, the Canadian market presents a unique opportunity to increase profits by repackaging the content that has already been produced for the U.S. market in a second edition that includes advertisements paid for by Canadian companies. Because they don't have to cover the cost of content (which is simply lifted from the U.S. edition), these split-run magazines can undercut their Canadian competitors on advertising rates. Years ago, the Canadian government recognized that if U.S. magazines were allowed to practice this "cultural dumping," there would not be a Canadian magazine industry. Faced with such unfair competition, the industry would inevitably wither away, no matter how good the quality of its product.

In October 1998, Canada responded to the WTO decision with new rules that target Canadian advertising in split-run magazines. Whether these new rules will withstand another complaint to the WTO or U.S. retaliation remains to be seen. What is clear, however, is that it is only a matter of time before the Americans, having won the 1997 case at the WTO, renew their attack on the other measures used by the federal government to maintain Canadian content in mass media. We may be successful in fighting a delaying action. In the long run, however, these trade law battles will be rendered moot by a technological development — the Internet.

The Internet will eventually make it impossible to enforce Canadian content restrictions on mass media. Until now, Canadian content regulations have been enforced at two principal points. Physical objects like magazines are controlled at the border (except when they are beamed by satellite into a Canadian press, as in the case of *Sports Illustrated*). Radio and television signals are controlled by means of a broadcast licence, which every Canadian broadcaster, including cable operators, must obtain. As a condition of that licence, broadcasters are required to report regularly on their compliance with Canadian content regulations. It is harder to control satellite broadcasters, but U.S.-based operators are required to refuse to provide the technology needed to descramble their signals to customers in Canada.

THE DILEMMA OF THE INTERNET

In the mid-1990s the set of technologies that we call the Internet emerged from its military and academic roots. Since then, the Internet has grown and expanded faster than any communications medium in history. Almost everyone who uses it can remember that feeling of excitement and awe when they first realized that, with one click of a mouse, they could access a computer in Japan. Or Australia. Or Singapore. Or the British Museum. Or the Louvre. Or . . . The possibilities are endless.

Initially, the Internet could deliver only text. Then came graphics. Then animation. Then sounds. Then moving pictures — that is, video. While it will still take several years to overcome the technical hurdles, it is only a matter of time before the Internet will be able to deliver on-demand music and video to the home. When that day arrives, the federal government's Canadian content regulations will be rendered obsolete.

In theory, it might be possible for the Canadian government to require

Internet service providers (ISPs) to install technology that would restrict the ability of Canadians to access certain types of content from outside Canada. In practice, however, this would be impossible. Canadians would correctly interpret this as an unacceptable restriction of their rights as protected under the Canadian Charter of Rights and Freedoms. Any federal government that attempted to restrict Canadians' rights in this way would be committing political suicide.

As noted earlier, Canadian content regulations are not designed to censor U.S. content. They are simply meant to ensure that the producers and distributors of mass media maintain a minimum level of Canadian content. However, when it comes to the global Internet, there is no intermediary between the consumer and the provider of content. Furthermore, unlike broadcasting, the Internet is a "pull" medium rather than a "push" medium. The programming decisions are, in effect, made by the consumer when he or she decides which websites to visit.

The Internet presents Canada with an enormous dilemma. On the one hand, it offers Canadians an unparalleled opportunity to communicate inexpensively with people around the world, and to access information that would previously have been impossible to find. On the other hand, the evidence is clear that the same U.S. corporations that dominate traditional mass media intend to dominate entertainment on the Internet as well. Canada can continue to subsidize Canadian creative production, but it will not be able to enforce content restrictions on the Internet.

Many will argue that this doesn't matter, that the Canadian cultural industries are now strong enough that they won't be drowned out by competition from the U.S. It is true that the Canadian cultural industries are stronger than ever before, and are successfully competing in the U.S. and elsewhere. However, the success of Canadian cultural industries in penetrating foreign markets depends on their maintaining a critical mass in Canada. That critical mass has been attained so far by the creation of a structure which ensures that Canadian media outlets are largely Canadian-owned, and that they broadcast or print a minimum amount of Canadian material. This guarantees that a minimum proportion of Canadian advertising dollars end up supporting production in Canada.

This structure will gradually be undermined by the delivery of mass media through the Internet. Within a few years, consumers will have access to entertainment sourced from websites anywhere in the world, and in many cases will pay for it directly using their credit cards. Canadian media outlets will no longer have, in effect, a captive audience to offer to Canadian advertisers.

Here's a taste of what is coming. The technology already exists that could enable, to give one example, the Walt Disney Corporation to recognize when a consumer from Canada is accessing its website, and automatically put up a banner ad from a Canadian advertiser. As pay-per-view over the Internet becomes technically feasible, Disney will be able to offer consumers a choice: watch *Snow White* uninterrupted for a small fee, or watch it for free with a minimum number of targeted advertisements from Canadian firms.

This technology will cut Canadian broadcasters out of the loop entirely. The pay-per-view fees and the advertising dollars will go directly to the U.S., and will not be used to support production in Canada. The Canadian government will be powerless to prevent this. It shouldn't prevent Canadian companies from advertising in the U.S., since it is entirely legitimate and necessary for them to do so if they want to access the U.S. market. And Canada cannot, and should not, prevent its citizens from receiving their entertainment directly from Walt Disney if they want to.

Of course, these same technologies will be available to Canada's cultural industries. But there is no Canadian company that will ever be able to come close to competing with the American entertainment giants when it comes to selection, share of mind, and the ability to spend unheard-of amounts of money on advertising and technology.

SO WHAT IS THE SOLUTION?

Paradoxically enough, the solution is SchoolNet. SchoolNet is a classic example of Internet's power to tap into the creativity of thousands of people. It was created to encourage schools to acquire access to the Internet, and to make learning resources available on the Net. Point your Web browser to www.schoolnet.ca and prepare to be amazed. For those without access, here's the description of SchoolNet from the Industry Canada website.

SCHOOLNET

What is it?

Canada's SchoolNet provides Canada's educators with on-line access to resources that help students acquire cutting-edge skills in Internet research and communication. As well, the SchoolNet Website offers users more than 1000 learning services and resources, including training and research tools.

Who's involved?

To provide all young Canadians with this resource, the federal government brought together a national advisory board of provincial and territorial governments, universities and colleges, educational associations, the telecommunications industry, and other private-sector representatives. It is a shining example of how partnership works to promote the effective use of information technology and ignite in young Canadians the interest to develop skills needed to compete in the knowledge-based economy.

How does it work?

Experience the excitement of classrooms without walls, information without limits, and communication without borders. SchoolNet is an unequalled set of educational resources for educators and learners all across our country.

> Students can easily find reliable facts on any topic they choose! There are interactive quizzes, projects and games that make learning fun. They can tour a virtual museum or zoo, sail around the world on an open-class 12 metre yacht, discover our First Nations heritage, talk to a Canadian astronaut in space, receive feedback from famous Canadian writers, artists and scientists on their work, study the migration of birds and insects and share these unique learning experiences with other students around the world!
>
> By the end of fiscal year 1998, SchoolNet will help ensure that all of Canada's 16,500 schools and 3,400 public libraries are connected to the Internet.
>
> Besides providing information, SchoolNet initiatives also perform the following services:
>
> - providing teachers with financial support to develop on-line projects;
> - finding the best buys in new computer hardware or software;
> - supplying training tools and services to help users access the Internet.
>
> To find out more, call 1-800-268-6608 or point your browser to: http://www.schoolnet.ca

SchoolNet is so multi-faceted that it is impossible to do it justice in print without going on for pages. However, here is just one example of its power.

One of its more recent programs is SchoolNet Digital Collections. Through this program, teams of young Canadians are funded to produce websites that feature significant Canadian material from the public domain, drawn from the collections of the National Library of Canada, the Canada Council, and hundreds of other repositories of Canadian heritage.

It was through SchoolNet that we were able to access the full text of the Massey-Lévesque report. Think about it. Here is a seminal Canadian document that was published almost fifty years ago. Someone living in St. John's or Victoria might be able to find a copy at a university library if he or she was lucky. Someone in Iqaluit wouldn't have a chance. Now, thanks to SchoolNet Digital Collections, any Canadian student — or anyone in the world with Internet access — can find the full text of the report. As Industry Minister John Manley has noted, "SchoolNet is helping to make Canada the most connected nation in the world."

The importance of this initiative is magnified when one realizes that for the Internet generation, if it's not on the Internet, it doesn't exist. Since it is so much more convenient to do research on the Internet than go to a library, there is a real risk that current and future generations of students will never become exposed to much of Canada's heritage if it's not available through the Internet.

In itself, SchoolNet is not a sufficient response to the challenge the Internet creates for Canadian cultural sovereignty. However, it points the way to what could be the answer: a National Project on educational new media.

THE STRATEGIC IMPORTANCE OF A NATIONAL PROJECT ON EDUCATIONAL NEW MEDIA

Educational new media (ENM) in this context means any educational material that is digital — that is, designed to be delivered via a computer. It could be distributed on a disk, a CD-ROM, a DVD, or the Internet. The term covers the full spectrum from preschool to adult education. It could be part of a formal school curriculum, training delivered on the job, or the kind of informal education that many people pursue out of interest and a desire to expand their horizons.

Educational new media will never replace traditional teacher-led education. But it will become an increasingly important component of formal education, training, and self-directed learning.

Why Is ENM Strategically Important for Canada?

ENM is important for several reasons.

1. First, it has a significant role to play in strengthening Canada's educational system. Good ENM challenges students, stimulates creativity, and provides feedback on student performance. Many teachers are already using ENM effectively, and they know that it can enable them to become more effective and productive. Some teachers have become authors of ENM themselves, and are seeing their work used more broadly within the educational system.

    However, there's a lot of schlock out there masquerading as ENM. There's an enormous opportunity to produce quality ENM designed to serve the needs of Canada's learners, whether children or adults. One of the essential characteristics of ENM, like software generally, is that the cost of producing a second copy is infinitely smaller than the cost of the first copy. Hence, it is logical to think about designing an ENM production system that can manufacture what we need for Canada and simultaneously adapt it for use in other countries as well.

    To make this possible, we need to create an effective partnership between Canadian educators and the creative professionals engaged in producing ENM materials. Each group needs the skills of the other to ensure that Canadian-produced ENM materials are effective and meet a high standard of excellence.

2. Second, ENM provides a way of implementing lifelong learning on a massive scale. Every major study of education in the last twenty-five years has recognized that we need to become a society of lifelong learners. We've made progress in this direction, but we are still far from where we need to be.

    One of the reasons that we have not yet been successful in shifting the focus of the educational system to lifelong learning, in addition to educating the young, is that it was too expensive to do this using traditional institution-based approaches to education. ENM offers another way to accomplish this objective.

3. Third, ENM could be a major source of high-quality, creative, knowledge worker jobs across the entire country. There's no reason why these jobs have to be concentrated in Toronto, Montreal, and Vancouver. The Internet lets ENM workers live anywhere.

As premier of New Brunswick, Frank McKenna showed Canadians that by pooling the resources of a province, and combining political leadership with good old-fashioned salesmanship, it is possible to attract the investment needed to create large numbers of knowledge worker jobs in areas that are almost entirely dependent on traditional resource industries.

There is already a large market for ENM, and this will continue to grow. A market assessment conducted by Industry Canada in 1996 showed that by 2005, the market for ENM in the business-training sector will be worth more than $2 billion in Canada alone. This does not include the two other major segments of the market, formal education and informal learning, and it doesn't include the international market. On a global basis, it's safe to predict that the market for ENM will soon be worth hundreds of billions of dollars.

We should set ourselves the target of obtaining a significant share of the global market for educational new media — somewhere in the range of 10 to 20 percent. This goal is essential because if we don't achieve a significant share of the global market, we won't have sufficient critical mass in Canada. In the long run, the ENM industry will be as important to our society and culture as cultural industries and mass media are today. However, if we don't achieve this critical mass, we won't be able to capture at least a 50 percent share of the domestic market, which is essential if we want to maintain Canadian culture.

4. Canada is well-positioned to compete in the ENM market. We have a large and successful film and video industry. We are a world leader in the deployment and use of telecommunications and distance education. We are already a major supplier of the specialized software used in video production and computer animation. We already have a

major market share in international video co-production. TV Ontario is already the largest distributor of educational programming in the U.S. Several Canadian organizations, such as Thomson International, are leaders in the North American information industry.

Canada has some unique advantages in the emerging international ENM market. We have ready access to the U.S. market. Outside the U.S., our experience with a dominant culture provides a basis for sensitivity to countries with similar concerns. We have a multicultural, multilingual society, full of people who are capable of producing content suitable for any country in the world, which is why IBM located one of its major software labs in Toronto. We are a significant player in both the Commonwealth and la Francophonie. Finally, we have an international reputation that makes us a credible supplier of educational resources.

5. A National Project on ENM creates a second way of maintaining the critical mass of skills and talent that is currently clustered around Canada's cultural industries. We're not suggesting that we should in any way abandon our existing cultural industries. Rather, we're observing that ENM draws on the same skills as the cultural industries: video production, software expertise, creative writing, graphic design, and so on. ENM provides an alternative way to fund the deployment of those skills, which are currently supported by using Canadian content regulations to channel advertising dollars into Canadian production. In other words, a major ENM strategy is an insurance policy for Canada's cultural industries.

It is also the best way to ensure that Canada's culture, history, and literature are there on the Internet for present and future generations of students, for Canadians in general, and for anyone else who wants to know more about us.

Some will wonder why, instead of concentrating on educational new media, we don't have a National Project on new media generally. It is true that there are major opportunities for Canada in new media beyond ENM. In fact, the ENM strategy will be synergistic with the development of the entire new media industry. And of course, we should pursue any opportunities to create good new media jobs. However, there are three reasons for focusing on ENM.

First, we're better off strategically focusing on ENM than going head to head with Disney and the other U.S. multimedia giants. Our slogan could be "Let the Americans Dominate Entertainment; We'll Be the Leaders in Education."

Second, our positioning in the international markets will be stronger if we clearly differentiate ourselves from the American multimedia edutainment industry, and become recognized as the source of the highest-quality ENM products. We should differentiate ourselves by our willingness to adapt and customize ENM resources to address local cultural sensitivities. After all, we know what it's like to live beside a dominant culture.

Third, given ENM's link to education and cultural policy, governments have a strategic and essential role to play, and can help create a competitive advantage for the Canadian industry. There are important ways that governments can, and should, help develop new media as a whole, but their role in this is necessarily less pervasive.

SOME POTENTIAL STRATEGIES

If we agree to launch a National Project on educational new media, here are some of the strategies we should consider:

1. We should continue to support Canada's cultural industries with appropriate funding and Canadian content regulations. Just because the latter are likely to come under attack doesn't mean we should give up.
2. ENM in Canada is rife with the potential for self-defeating turf protection. The provinces control education. There's a dispute about who

controls training. For some reason, the British North America Act made no mention of new media.

The best way to overcome this problem is with real, live international contracts. (There's nothing that pulls various organizations together better than the prospect of new incremental revenue.) Consequently, we should build on our experience with the national organization that was set up to market Canada's health expertise overseas: Interhealth (http://www.interhealth.com). This consortium was established with the support of several provincial governments (in fact, the initiative came from Ontario, with help from the imaginative MDS corporation) and the private sector, and eventually got some federal support. It's a successful model we could adapt to help market Canada's ENM expertise overseas.

The ENM export strategy should also build on the educational marketing initiatives already undertaken by the Department of Foreign Affairs and International Trade and the Canadian International Information Strategy, promoted by Foreign Affairs Minister Lloyd Axworthy.

3. As part of our marketing strategy, we need to create a comprehensive Internet-based catalogue of all Canadian ENM resources. Knowledge Connection Corporation of Toronto has already started this process, which could be expanded and made fully national in scope.

4. One effective way to market Canada's ENM materials is to create an Internet portal that effectively organizes the information and resources on the global Internet that relate to ENM.

To understand what we mean by this, consider the example of Strategis (http://strategis.ic.gc.ca). Remember Nicholson's First Law, quoted in Chapter 6: The competitive advantage of government is knowledge. Industry Canada apparently took this to heart, and created Strategis, which is a remarkable accomplishment and an astonishingly useful resource for business. Strategis is a gateway, or portal, to all the information that Industry Canada has collected about the

Canadian and global economies in recent years. It also includes information from other government departments. Using the power of information technology, Strategis provides access to this information in a variety of ways — by subjects and categories, keyword searches, etc. In essence, Strategis is a portal to the entire information base of the federal government as it relates to business.

There's an opportunity for Canada to use a similar technological approach to create the best portal in the world to information about ENM. The ENM portal would soon become the first place anyone on the planet would go if they were looking for information or resources about ENM. Naturally, many of these resources would be from the Canadian catalogue, but we should provide links to good resources wherever they might be found. That's how we will know what the competition is up to, and how we can keep ahead.

If we do this right, all ENM roads on the Internet will lead to Canada.

5. There are a number of key areas on which the provincial and federal governments need to collaborate.

Standards: We need to establish national quality standards for ENM and to ensure some level of cross-platform compatibility.

Procurement: The provinces and the federal government should recognize the strategic importance of having a strong ENM industry in Canada, and should use procurement policy to help this industry grow. Properly approached, this will not violate our commitments under NAFTA or other international trade agreements. Procurement could be effectively applied in primary, secondary, and post-secondary institutions, in government purchases to meet internal training requirements, and in ENM purchases in support of lifelong learning.

Financing: Governments have a role to play in making sure that financing is available for ENM production companies and for specific projects.

Explicit lifelong learning strategy: Governments should

develop explicit strategies with respect to lifelong learning, and ensure that Canadians have access to relevant ENM resources.

Equitable access to high-speed networking: A major inequity at present is that urban Canadians have high-speed Internet access through cable, ISDN (integrated services digital network), LMCS (local multi-point channel services), and ADSL (asymmetrical digital sub-scriber line). Generally speaking, Canadians in rural areas are limited to Internet access over phone modems at speeds that are ten to fifty times slower than the new technologies. The federal government has done a good job so far ensuring that all Canadian communities have some form of Internet access. However, to meet our societal goals, all Canadians must have access to high-speed links. If we want ENM jobs to be spread out across the country, and not concentrated in the big cities, this is essential.

With previous communications technologies — mail and the tele-phone — government policies ensured that Canadians in small towns and rural and remote areas were not at a disadvantage. A similar approach will be necessary with respect to high-speed networking, since the private sector won't offer equitable access unless they are forced to. Bell Canada, for example, has admitted that it doesn't expect to offer high-speed services in rural Ontario any time soon. This needs to change.

ENM intellectual property clearinghouse: Securing the right to use material from public and private sources is one of the biggest challenges facing teachers and entrepreneurs developing ENM. The federal government should create an ENM intellectual property clear-inghouse that would assist Canadians in obtaining the rights to mate-rials to be included in ENM projects. A national clearinghouse would have the ability to negotiate better deals with foreign sources than indi-vidual Canadians negotiating on their own. This is particularly impor-tant because Bill Gates and others have already used their economic clout to acquire the electronic rights to the contents of major museums and art collections around the world. An efficient and effective rights-clearing process could give an enormous competitive advantage to Canadian ENM developers.

Incentives for teachers: Provincial governments should ensure that proper incentives exist to encourage teachers to participate in ENM projects, and that they are appropriately recognized and rewarded for doing so.

6. Universities also have an important role to play with respect to ENM. In addition to research and technology development, they should be encouraged to develop courseware that can be used across the country and exported around the world.

   In an important initiative, the federal government provided funding in 1995 for the TeleLearning Network of Centres of Excellence (http://www.telelearn.ca), headquartered at Simon Fraser University. The TeleLearning Network is supported by all three of Canada's research councils, by Industry Canada, and by more than seventeen industrial sponsors. It links more than 130 researchers in thirty universities across Canada. This and similar initiatives, such as provincial centres of excellence, need continuing support.

7. In the Third World, education is the single most important tool for development. The best thing Canada can do to help developing countries is to provide support for education. The most effective thing we can do to support education is to help developing countries acquire ENM materials, both hardware and software, and in so doing, enable their teachers to stretch their time and their resources, both of which are currently in short supply. Given the opportunity, children in developing countries will prove to be just as quick as Canadian kids to latch on to the potential of the Internet.

   The Canadian International Development Agency and the International Development Research Centre are familiar with these opportunities, but they have lacked both the resources and the focus to enable our international ENM efforts to reach their full potential. As part of a National Project on educational new media, however, support for ENM could be a focal point of our international development activities.

8. To coordinate the project on educational new media, we need a national network that will encourage collaboration among educators, the private sector, the provincial and federal governments, the CBC, provincial educational broadcasters, and the cultural industries generally. SchoolNet already offers a nucleus around which the broader network could be organized. There are other existing organizations that could be involved, including the Canadian Network for New Media Learning, the New Brunswick–based Centre international pour le developpement de l'inforoute en français, and the Association for Media and Technology in Education in Canada. In principal cities across Canada there are other potential participants, some of whom don't focus entirely on educational new media. They include: MEDIAfusion (Halifax); Centre d'expertise et de services en applications multimédias and Forum des inforoutes et du multimédia (Montreal); OCRI and New Media North Consortium (Ottawa); Knowledge Connection Corporation, Knowledge Media Design Institute, SMART Toronto, and Interactive Multimedia Arts and Technologies Association (Toronto); New Media West (Winnipeg); Saskatchewan New Media Developers Association (Regina); Edmonton New Media Initiative and Alberta Association of Courseware Producers (Edmonton); and New Media B.C. (Vancouver).

Another major role of the national network should be to encourage and facilitate local initiatives. The power of the ENM strategy can best be unleashed by supporting a large number of community-based initiatives. Each participating community should be provided with the resources and support needed to develop its own ENM strategy, which should address financing, school/college/university/business linkages and networks, infrastructure, staffing, and local lifelong learning programs.

The importance and power of community initiatives was reinforced for us when we helped to launch a new-media initiative centred in the former Borough of East York, in John Godfrey's riding of Don Valley West. In the mid-1990s, East York faced the prospect of a major setback as, one by one, major employers in the old Leaside industrial area closed or moved their operations elsewhere. During the search for ways to offset the potential decline in the local job market and the tax base, the idea emerged that the borough could position itself as a centre for new media activity in Toronto. We discovered that East York already had the largest concentration of graphic artists in Toronto, and that it had the best access to high-speed networks in the metropolitan region. It was also home to the Bell Centre for Creative Communications at Centennial College.

With the help of Mayor Michael Prue, Conservative MPP John Parker, and local councillors, we organized a series of community meetings in John Godfrey's riding office to explore this idea further. At the first meeting, there were eight people around the table. At the second meeting, two weeks later, there were sixteen people. At the third meeting, a month later, there were thirty people. The fourth meeting, a few weeks later, was standing-room only — more than sixty people had showed up. Subsequent meetings were moved to the more spacious council chamber of the East York municipal offices.

The next step was to organize a series of task forces to develop an overall strategy. Dozens of people volunteered their time, and eventually the New Media Village Growth Corporation was created. As noted on the New Media Village website (http://www.newmediavillage.com), "New Media Village Growth Corporation supports the growth of New Media companies by providing financial contacts, education linkages and high speed bandwidth. The New Media Village is a private-public partnership funded by corporate sponsors which include firms from the financial services industry, real estate development community, new media sector, the City of Toronto and Human Resources Development Canada."

New Media Village is still expanding. It not only survived the forced amalgamation of East York and Toronto's other suburbs, but it is now spreading its wings to encourage the growth of new media clusters in eight areas across the new mega-city. The innovative website offers a unique method for new media firms to access all types of financing assistance; it also presents real-estate companies with an exciting way to showcase their bandwidth-ready buildings, in both two- and three-dimensional formats.

The lesson of New Media Village is that, given the opportunity, Canadians will respond with both time and money when it comes to helping their communities. Too often, we haven't created that opportunity. National Projects can furnish both the leadership and the support structures needed to unleash and leverage the power of local initiatives.

10

A National Project for Y2K

The previous four chapters have been about positive National Projects — ones that we should undertake to move Canada's society and economy forward. This chapter is about a National Project that may be required to avert a disaster caused primarily by the private sector, and where government regulatory action to eliminate this predictable and preventable threat was missing.

As this book went to press, millions of computer programmers around the globe were engaged in a desperate race against time — to ensure that the world's computers continued to function properly on January 1, 2000.

By now, most people are aware that in the early years of computing, programmers were under pressure to save storage space, and so recorded dates using only two digits for the year. Instead of 31/3/1999, for example, they used 31/3/99. Unless this problem is fixed, computers will be confused on January 1, 2000, since 1/1/00 could refer to either the year 2000 or the year 1900. This problem is referred to by a number of names — Y2K (which stands for year 2000), the Millennium Bug, and so on.

Calculations using times and dates are widespread in computing. They are used to coordinate machinery within a factory, to maintain maintenance schedules, for navigation purposes in ships and planes, to track the shelf life of perishables, to control security systems, to calculate interest in banking, to flag due dates for financial obligations, and for billing purposes in energy and communications, to cite only a few examples. If the date problems in software and embedded chips are not corrected, there is a risk of service interruptions in the fundamental systems that underlie our society and economy: energy, communications, banking, transportation, health care, and so on.

The Canadian government has launched a major effort to ensure that government computers are "year 2000 compliant," and has created a task force to encourage the private sector to do the same. The task force regularly reports on progress, but also notes that much work remains to be done.

It is impossible to know precisely what the impacts of the Millennium Bug will be. We don't know how many systems will be fixed by December 31, 1999. We don't know whether the fixes will be complete, or whether there will remain undetected problems that will emerge on or after January 1, 2000. We don't know to what extent problems elsewhere in the world may affect our infrastructure and economy.

Given the level of risk and uncertainty, the correct response is to plan for contingencies. The Canadian government is taking this responsibility seriously. The military has launched Operation Abacus, which is a comprehensive program of coordination with federal and provincial authorities to ensure that appropriate emergency measures can be taken if there are significant problems in the early days and weeks of the year 2000. Under Operation Abacus, the military will pre-position supplies, equipment, and personnel at strategic locations throughout the country, ready to offer emergency assistance if required.

The Royal Canadian Mounted Police has told its staff to forget about holidays in the first few months of the year 2000. Other police forces and emergency services across the country are considering taking similar action.

The Bank of Canada has announced that it will increase the supply of printed money to allow for the fact that many citizens will choose to accumulate extra cash in late 1999 in case there is an interruption in banking services in the year 2000.

Similar contingency planning operations are taking place throughout the country, and more can be expected as 1999 unfolds.

The problem Canadians need to face, however, is that even if computer systems in Canada are largely fixed by the year 2000, or even if the problems that occur are minor and their impact limited by appropriate contingency responses, we may encounter a major economic disruption caused by problems in other parts of the world.

It is generally recognized, for example, that Europe is well behind North America in making its systems year 2000 compliant, mainly because its programmers were engaged in another major task — preparing for the introduction of the new European currency, the Euro, on January 1, 1999. Countries in Asia were distracted by the severe economic recession that swept through the region beginning in mid-1997, and that then spilled over into Eastern Europe and South America as well. Developing countries in general have been slow to recognize the potential disruptions that may occur in their power grids and telecommunications systems.

By the fall of 1998, the entire world economy seemed shaky, with volatile stock markets, a massive "flight to quality" in currency markets, and widespread misery as emerging middle classes in many developing countries were plunged back into poverty. The year 2000 problem could put the world economy over the edge into a global depression.

Many people around the world are working to ensure that this doesn't happen. We hope they succeed. However, we think the risk of economic problems is sufficiently great that some contingency planning is appropriate. The purpose of this chapter, therefore, is to consider how Canada should respond in the event that the year 2000 problem does result in a major economic disruption.

If this occurs, we will need a National Project on recovery from the year 2000 computer bug.

THE GOALS OF A NATIONAL PROJECT ON RECOVERY FROM THE YEAR 2000 COMPUTER BUG

The first goal should be to ensure that appropriate responses are made to any problems that threaten the lives of Canadians. The second goal should be to coordinate remedial action to get any mission-critical computers that fail back on-line as quickly as possible, and to restore any interruptions in basic services such as energy, water, communications, and health care. We make the assumption that contingency planning to address these problems is well underway, and therefore we won't examine them further.

The third goal should be to do as much as possible to protect Canadians from the consequences of a problem that was not of their making. It is important to emphasize that the private sector "owns" this problem. The year 2000 computer bug is not like a hurricane or other "act of God." This is an entirely man-made problem, which was predictable, and was predicted, with a deadline that was known well in advance. The information technology industry, which created the problem in the first place, has known about it for decades. Major corporations also had plenty of warning about the problem and its consequences. Most neglected to allocate resources to fix it until it was almost too late — and for some, it already is too late.

Governments, of course, have a responsibility to fix their own computers. But the year 2000 computer bug can't be blamed on government. One could argue that governments should have recognized years ago that the private sector was not taking action quickly enough to solve the problem, and should have passed legislation to force companies to allocate resources earlier. In the atmosphere of the early 1990s, however, such government action would have been considered as inappropriate meddling in the private sector's domain.

Since the private sector owns this problem, it will have to allocate the resources to fix it, and to ensure that individual Canadians do not suffer because of it.

In the early months of the year 2000, the federal government will need to equip itself with the powers to guarantee that no Canadian loses his or her savings or home because of the year 2000 problem. It must ensure that corporations put the needs of Canadian citizens, and not the needs of their shareholders, first. Then, with policies to protect individual Canadians in place, the federal and provincial governments must ensure that they will be in a position to help Canadian businesses recover as quickly as possible.

If there are major disruptions elsewhere in the world, many businesses that are dependent on imports for their raw materials or supplies will have difficulty operating. Canadian governments could help such businesses locate other sources of supplies. It may be necessary to do a major study of import substitute possibilities, identifying supply chains that might be interrupted and locating alternative local sources where possible.

Similarly, Canadian companies dependent on exporting outside North America may find their ability to ship overseas constrained by communication or transportation problems, or by the inability of their customers to pay. Canadian governments could mobilize resources to assist these companies. In some cases, it may be possible to find customers elsewhere in Canada.

Canadian governments may need to use our worldwide network of embassies and consulates in creative ways to help coordinate imports and exports that normally take place without government involvement. We may need to find an appropriate balance between agricultural production directed at local needs and emergency relief directed at other areas of the world. We may need to use powers similar to those last used during the

Second World War to coordinate and finance production to meet the needs of Canadians. Disruptions in communications and financial systems in other parts of the world may force us to consider barter or countertrade on a massive basis.

If there are significant economic problems, the natural response of governments will be to try to conserve resources and to cut back. However, this would be making the same mistake that governments in Canada made in the early 1930s. The single most important message of this chapter is that the best antidote to a major economic disruption would be to press ahead with National Projects — all the ones described in this book, and more besides.

We hope that these actions will never be necessary. If they are, we hope that the federal and provincial governments will be ready.

REGULATING TECHNOLOGY

Whatever the outcome of the year 2000 computer bug, this issue is a salutary reminder of the fact that the same technologies that offer great benefits may bring great risks as well.

Computers have brought tremendous benefits to the factory, the office, the school, the hospital, and the home. One of the things the year 2000 computer bug has accomplished is to remind us how dependent we are on computer technology. This dependence will continue long after the year 2000. While we will never again in our lifetimes face another Y2K-type problem, there are many other risks — from terrorists to ice storms — that could threaten the computer networks that have become mission-critical for our society. We need to think carefully about these risks and plan appropriately.

For example, it is completely predictable that some day foreign terror-ists will seek to inflict economic damage on North America by attacking our information networks. The United States recently launched a signifi-cant new initiative to defend itself against information warfare. Canadians deserve to know what actions we are taking at a national level to protect our own networks.

The year 2000 computer bug has also taught us that the private sector cannot be relied on to manage these risks adequately. There are many responsible companies that will make the year 2000 deadline. Taken as a whole, however, the private sector allocated too few resources, too late in the day, to respond to an issue that was perfectly predictable and had a clear deadline — December 31, 1999. How many of the other major technological risks out there have less predictability in the outcome and no clear deadline? There are still many in the field of computing. There are many more in the relatively young fields of biotechnology and genetics.

To cite but one example, some seed companies are currently working on technology that would ensure that the resulting plants are sterile. This is to prevent farmers from buying seed once, then collecting seed from the first year's crops to plant the following year. The seed companies want the farmers to have to buy new seed every year.

What are the risks this technology creates for our global society? Is there a chance that it could mutate unexpectedly and contaminate a whole plant species throughout the world? The truth is, we don't know. The seed company doesn't know. The farmer doesn't know. Our government doesn't know.

In November 1998, people around the world were concerned about the potential impact of the Leonid meteor shower on the world's satellite network. As it turned out, the impact was less than many people had feared. However, the point is that until it happened, we didn't know what to expect. Because of our dismal track record with respect to the environmental impact of our actions, environmentalists now talk about the "precautionary principle" — the right response to a lack of knowledge is not to assume the best, but rather to assume we should at least exercise caution.

The private sector has no incentive to consider such questions in a comprehensive and balanced way. To say this is not to attack the private sector. Comprehensive risk assessment from a societal point of view is not the primary responsibility of corporations. In the eyes of most private sector executives, their job is to develop new products and services that have benefits for their customers, introduce them to the marketplace, operate efficiently, and maximize returns for their owners, the shareholders.

One can argue that companies have a responsibility to society at large, given the benefits they derive from that society. We believe that markets serve society, not the other way round. We believe that the market system happens to be an extraordinarily effective way to get certain things done. We wouldn't want to live without it. But society needs government to regulate the functioning of markets to ensure that in the end, the broad interests of society prevail over the narrower interests of market participants.

The biggest mistake that Russia and other members of the former Soviet bloc made was to assume that all they had to do to realize the benefits of capitalism was to install markets. They didn't realize that markets work well in Western countries because they operate within a complex framework of institutions and regulations that, more or less successfully, define the boundaries within which markets can operate to the benefit of society at large.

Corporations will usually resist these constraints, although occasionally we see entire industries begging for regulations to protect them from stronger competitors. If asked, the boards of directors of corporations will assert, with complete sincerity, that they take social responsibility seriously. In the final analysis, however, the performance of the vast majority of executives is evaluated not on the basis of social responsibility, but on increases in profits and share price. There are initiatives underway that have the potential to introduce a broader set of performance indicators — notably the Canadian Performance Reporting Initiative of the Canadian Institute of Chartered Accountants. At present, however, profits and share price rule.

The task of assessing the risks posed by new technologies, and ensuring that markets and technologies are regulated properly, can be performed only by government. Under pressure from budget deficits, governments in Canada and around the world have been reducing the resources allocated to technology risk assessment and regulation. The Republicans in the U.S. Congress killed the Office of Technology Assessment. Mulroney's Conservatives killed the Science Council of Canada. Mike Harris killed the Ontario Premier's Council.

Many Canadians are concerned that the Health Protection Branch at Health Canada has been weakened by budget cuts, and that private sector interests are playing too large a role in the process of determining what products are safe. Questions linger about whether we should have foreseen the risks to the Atlantic and Pacific fisheries sooner, and whether we are smart to continue to practice monoculture on the Prairies to such an extent.

If the year 2000 computer bug teaches us anything, it is that government must not shirk its responsibility to be the watchdog for society. How do we ensure that governments are allocating sufficient resources to this task? Perhaps this is a role for the auditor general of Canada and the provincial auditors. We'd like to see these issues explored in a conference in the spring of the year 2000 so that we will never again have to contemplate a National Project to avert a man-made disaster.

In the meantime, if you know any programmers working on the year 2000 bug, bake them a casserole, buy them a double espresso, and promise them a good time if they get the job done by New Year's Eve.

Choosing National Projects

How do we choose which National Projects we should pursue? This chapter proposes a set of criteria that we believe all National Projects should meet, and points towards other potential National Projects that we hope Canadians will decide to explore in subsequent discussions.

CRITERIA FOR NATIONAL PROJECTS

All National Projects should meet the following five criteria (which we believe are met by the projects described in Chapters 6 through 9).

1. They should offer benefits to Canadian society as a whole, and should not be directed at a particular group or region. We should focus on the developmental health of all Canadians and all children, not just Canadians in the West or children who are disadvantaged in some way. This does not mean that we should not implement policies directed at

regions or groups — only that such initiatives should not be confused with National Projects.

2. National Projects should be knowledge-based — that is, founded on sound science or technology or both. For example, it is our understanding of the science underlying human development that forces us to shift our focus from traditional health care to the broader concept of developmental health.

3. National Projects should have the potential to deliver measurable outcomes that will significantly enhance quality of life and well-being for Canadians. We shouldn't implement any National Project before we have defined what outcomes we are trying to achieve, and how we will measure our success in achieving those outcomes.

4. National Projects should have significant positive benefits for Canada's long-run competitive position in the global economy. Points 3 and 4 reflect the insight demonstrated by former Ontario premier Bob Rae in a powerful speech made to members of the Ontario Premier's Councils as they began their work together in June 1991. The speech was entitled "Building a Common Sense." (In light of subsequent events, Ontarians will appreciate the irony of this title.)

> One of the illusions of our time is that there is this great battle between those people who believe in equity and those people who believe in efficiency. We are constantly being told that government has to choose either to support equity or to support efficiency. Either you talk the language of competitiveness and productivity and efficiency and you follow policies which will produce that, or, we are told, you talk the language of equality and social policy and of greater equity and of greater social justice and you deal with those. They are at odds with one another.
>
> We are told that we either have to follow the policies of those governments which have chosen the path of focusing all their energies and directions on greater growth, or those who have

chosen, rather, to stress the importance of a greater equality. To put it bluntly, you are either in support of wealth creation, or you are in support of wealth distribution, but you cannot be in support of both.

I am here to tell you, and you are here to tell me for the next several years, but tonight I am here to tell you, that I think that is nonsense. I think that it is nonsense, a myth that has to be rooted out and that we have to deal with as people. I think, in fact, that if you ask people what they want in our country, what they believe is fair, what they think is realistic, they in fact believe in both. They do not think it is unfair or unrealistic for our society, governments, business, everyone else, to believe in both as well.

Rae's insight is illustrated by the National Projects described in this book. If we do a good job on developmental health, our society will be more productive and competitive. Chapter 7 demonstrates that there are many ways in which Canada would achieve a positive return on an investment in readiness to learn. The new energy systems and educational new media projects have great wealth-creation potential as well as great societal benefits. We should insist that all National Projects have both an economic return and other societal benefits.

This is also the fundamental response to those who are concerned that National Projects will lead us back into the Valley of the Shadow of Deficits. Having finally, after twenty years, clawed our way out of that valley, we are not inclined to jump back in. However, the desire to avoid deficits should not prevent us from being willing, as a society, to make sensible investments that promise an economic return as well as societal benefits. Like any businessperson, we should be disciplined in estimating those potential economic returns prior to undertaking any National Project, and we should measure progress along the way to ensure that we achieve them. But we also have to be prepared to take calculated risks.

5. All National Projects should have a positive transformative effect on one or more of Canada's major societal systems. This requires some further explanation.

SYSTEMIC CHANGE

The concept of systemic change in societal systems provides a useful alternative perspective for thinking about National Projects. It can be argued that Canada, like other industrialized countries, has eight major societal systems. These include:

1. *The economic system*, which consists of a multitude of firms and organizations connected to each other through supplier, customer, and other collaborative relationships.
2. *The health care system*, which includes hospitals, clinics, and other medical establishments; public health agencies; doctors; health research organizations; and the private sector firms involved in developing and delivering various health-related products and services.
3. *The education system*, which includes primary and secondary schools, daycare and early childhood education agencies, post-secondary colleges and universities, public and private sector organizations delivering training, and the many private sector firms involved in various education and training-related activities.
4. *The social welfare system*, which includes a host of community and government agencies that provide the services collectively described as the "social safety net."
5. *The justice system*, which includes police services, the court system and related agencies, the prison system, and alternative dispute resolution mechanisms.
6. *The defence system*, which includes the armed forces; related civilian agencies; and the private sector firms furnishing weapons, supplies, and services.

7. *The system of physical infrastructure*, which includes the public and private sector organizations involved in providing transportation, communications, and related services.

8. *The science and technology infrastructure*, which includes research organizations in government, universities, and the private sector; agencies involved in setting technical standards; organizations involved in disseminating scientific and technological knowledge; etc.

All of these societal systems overlap to some extent, and are interlinked through the institutions that govern society, as depicted in the following diagram.

©Rob McLean, 1993

All of these major societal systems are today under pressure for change in Canada, and in many other societies as well. Some of this pressure results from the need to minimize the tax burden on citizens. However, even in the absence of fiscal pressures, it is evident that many of these systems need to evolve to a new stage of development. This is what we mean by "systemic change," and is why each National Project should have a transformative effect on these major societal systems.

To illustrate this point, let's focus on the health care system. Chapter 3 provided a brief outline of how Canadians got public health insurance, and noted that the Canadian system is systemically more efficient than the American private health insurance system. Looking more broadly at the health care system, we can see that it comprises a number of major components, any of which could theoretically be organized as private or public sector. The principal components are hospitals (public in Canada and largely private in the U.S.), doctors (most are private entrepreneurs in both countries), health insurance (public in Canada and mainly private in the U.S.), the drug industry (private in both countries), diagnostic services (mainly private in both countries), medical devices and supplies (private in both countries), and so on.

The debate should not be about whether the overall system should be private or public, but about which components should be private or public. No serious person has ever suggested that the medical drug industry should be anything other than private sector. What the private sector is incredibly good at is innovation and differentiation. The public sector is not particularly good at either, but a properly organized public sector service can be very efficient. If you want a health insurance system that delivers a broad range of products, catering differentially to the wealthy versus the poor, then the private sector is the way to go. However, if what you want is to provide equitable access for all to the health care system, then it turns out, as explained in Chapter 3, that a public sector approach is far more efficient.

The challenge for a society, through its government, is to make intelligent choices about how best to evolve the health care system. It is not intelligent, as some provincial governments are doing, to promote privatization of public services based on ideologically driven assumptions about the relative efficiency of private versus public sector approaches. This would be true even if the only issue was how to maintain the existing system. It is doubly true when we also face the challenge of engineering systemic change.

In Chapter 6, we described the systemic change needed for the health system as shifting our focus to developmental health. This requires a set of proactive policies to encourage health in the population, along with effective funding and management of health care. A specific example of the application of these concepts to Canada's children is provided in Chapter 7. As we proceed down this path, we will need to carefully consider how we could benefit from the relative strengths of the private and the public sectors.

The National Project on new energy systems in Chapter 8 addresses some aspects of the challenge that exists with respect to physical infrastructure. The imperative is to ensure that our major infrastructures — energy, communications, and transportation — support competitiveness in a way that is compatible with sustainable development. There is clearly additional work to be done.

With respect to the education system, it is widely recognized that most Canadians in the workforce will be involved in a process of lifelong learning, given the continuous technological and organizational change that characterizes today's work environment. The need for lifelong learning has been anticipated in future-oriented public policy studies for two decades or more. However, we are still in only the very early stages of shifting from an educational system that is mainly focused on educating the young in batches of thirty or so to a system that caters to the needs of individuals engaged in a process of lifelong learning. Chapter 9 describes a project that will help with the systemic change needed in education. However, it is by no means a complete response.

OTHER POTENTIAL NATIONAL PROJECTS

By thinking about the need for systemic change in major societal systems, we can dimly recognize other potential National Projects that are not explored in this book, but that could usefully be the subject of further analysis and development.

We clearly don't have in Canada a consensus about the systemic changes needed in the social welfare system. Nobody is satisfied at present that we're allocating the right amount of resources, or that we have achieved the right balance between providing support and encouraging interdependence (we use the term "interdependence" because, for many people, true independence is not an option; interdependence, to us, conveys elements of independence as well as the recognition that we are all, to greater or lesser degrees, dependent on each other). We know that some municipalities and some provinces are doing a better job than others. We think there is probably an opportunity for a National Project here that would identify and build on the best approaches across Canada.

The systemic change needed for the justice system is to shift the emphasis from punishment to prevention of crime. The concept of crime prevention is not new. It is partially addressed by the National Project for Canada's children in Chapter 7. However, the resources in the justice system are still overwhelmingly allocated to police, lawyers, courts, and prisons. Perhaps we need a National Project that would identify the systemic changes needed if we truly want to prevent crime. In addition, we know that there are sectors of Canadian society where achieving even a modicum of social justice requires a major national effort — Canada's aboriginal peoples come to mind.

With respect to the defence system, it is generally recognized that the major external threats to the future security of Canadians come not from the military forces of other countries, but from terrorism, ecosystem destruction, and epidemics of drug-resistant microbes. While this reality has been recognized by Foreign Affairs Minister Lloyd Axworthy, and various related activities are underway, we have not yet implemented a fully comprehensive security strategy for Canadians. Perhaps the National Project approach has something to contribute here.

The systemic change required for the science and technology infrastructure is to shift the focus from research and development to innovative solutions. In past decades, the main aim of Canada's science policy, to the extent that there was one, was to increase spending on research and development (R&D), which in Canada was felt to be insufficient. It is now apparent that while R&D is important, it is more important to focus on innovative solutions to real societal problems (which are outputs, whereas R&D is an input). Focusing on innovative solutions leads to a more complex analysis of the roles of various institutions in the process of addressing the challenges facing Canadians and our global society.

Innovation is also the challenge with respect to the economy as a whole. The pressure here is to shift our policy focus to include innovation that crosses the boundaries between customers and suppliers, in addition to innovation within individual firms. In the mid-1980s, a group of radical economists broke away from the mainstream of the economics profession and began focusing attention on the innovation process at the national level. Through a series of projects, several of which were sponsored by the Paris-based Organization for Economic Co-operation and Development (OECD), they explored the implications of what we now refer to as "systems of innovation." Their approach was to consider the combined interactions of firms, universities, centres of excellence, government labs, technical standards bodies, the science and technology policy agencies, and other relevant organizations. While the Canadian government has been made aware of this approach, it has yet to implement it in a comprehensive way.

Canada's lack of an innovation strategy that spans the private and public sectors is the root cause of lower-than-expected productivity gains in recent years. This issue has recently been taken up by the business press, which was stimulated in part by an OECD report that pointed out that without greater gains in productivity on a year-over-year basis, Canadians run the risk of seeing their standard of living fall compared with other industrialized countries.

In order to understand the productivity problem, we need to lump firms into three categories that reflect their strategies for increasing productivity, which for purposes of this discussion may be defined as total revenue divided by the number of employees. In the first category are firms that simply reduce the number of employees without doing anything to increase revenue, resulting in higher profits and higher productivity.

The second category includes firms whose primary strategy is growth through merger or consolidation. If you buy or merge with another company in the same line of business, you will always have opportunities to improve efficiency and downsize staff in the resulting larger business. The combined revenues of the two firms are produced by a smaller number of employees, resulting in higher productivity. The growth of Conrad Black's newspaper empire is a classic illustration of this approach, as was the attempt of Canada's major banks to merge.

The third category includes firms whose primary strategy is to increase productivity through innovation that creates added value for customers, resulting in higher revenues being produced by the same or a higher number of employees. Ballard Power is a classic example of a firm whose strategy is growth through innovation.

Canada's current productivity problem is that over the past decade, since we began implementing the Free Trade Agreement, we have had too many firms in the first and second categories, and not enough in the third. From a national perspective, the problem with firms in the first and second categories is that their individual efforts to increase productivity tend to decrease employment, putting downward pressure on productivity at a national level. The Mulroney government never developed the active adjustment strategies promised during the free trade debate, and the current Liberal government, while it has taken some steps in the right direction, has not yet launched a comprehensive National Project to strengthen Canada's innovation systems.

GOVERNANCE

Governance is at the centre of our major societal systems. The word "governance" doesn't just mean government. All institutions have a process of governance, be it a board of directors of a corporation or not-for-profit organization, a school board, a university or college council of governors, or whatever. Governance is the process by which we set direction and evaluate performance for institutions and for society as a whole. The main challenge we face with governance is to escape the limitations of existing institutional structures. We described earlier the difficulty governments have in addressing issues that cross the boundaries between departments or the boundaries between different levels of government. The same applies to problems that cross the boundaries between the private and the public sectors generally.

That is why we need National Projects and Strategic Opportunities. To persuade people to take the risk of working across organizational boundaries, to tackle the whole problem and not just their piece of it, requires a vision that is powerful enough to overcome institutional inertia. It takes people who are committed enough to the vision that they will risk the ridicule of their peers and persist in what seems like an impossible task. Systemic change is not easy.

Fortunately, we are in the position of being able to learn from our past successes as a society — the six major National Projects of the 1950s, 1960s, and 1970s, which were described in Chapter 3. From our history, we learn that there are three critical ingredients, and without these no National Project or Strategic Opportunity can get off the ground.

The first is leadership. Each of our past successes required leadership from both the prime minister of Canada and the provincial premiers. St. Laurent, Diefenbaker, Pearson, and Trudeau all took significant risks at critical times to push these projects forward. So did people like Leslie Frost and Bill Davis in Ontario, Jean Lesage and Daniel Johnson Sr. in Quebec, Tommy Douglas in Saskatchewan, and Louis Robichaud in New Brunswick.

The second is vision. Time and again, we have seen that National Projects were launched based on the work of royal commissions led by reflective Canadians who dedicated themselves to reaching a deep understanding of both problems and possibilities. Fortunately, we still have such people working in the public interest, among them Fraser Mustard, who is the inspiration for many of the ideas in this book.

The third is resources. Nothing can be done without the willingness to allocate sufficient dollars to achieve worthy objectives in the public interest. The most important achievement of the present federal government to date is that Canada is again in a position to do that.

The Canada We Want: Reprise

The Canada We Want stands in sharp contrast to the future promoted by Conrad Black and Ian Angell, and to the dark visions of William Gibson.

It is a Canada in which governments, the private sector, and the institutions of civil society collaborate in a set of bold initiatives to create a better future for all members of society. In Chapters 6 through 11, we have attempted to describe what some of those initiatives might be.

No one of these initiatives by itself could successfully counteract the powerful forces that have been unleashed by globalization. As this book went to press, our vulnerability to external events was being demonstrated again: the Canadian dollar tested new lows, the Japanese government attacked the Canada-U.S. Auto Pact through the World Trade Organization, stock market volatility unnerved investors, British Columbia slid into a recession caused by the weakness in the Asian markets, and Canadian wheat and hog farmers faced the bleakest outlook since the Great Depression.

Since the mid-1970s, Canada has been living through a set of wrenching changes. During each of the last twenty-five years, at least one major sector of the Canadian economy has been in crisis. Forestry, the fishery, oil and gas, mining, agriculture, manufacturing, and retail have all at some point during the past two decades experienced major downturns. Each region of the country has endured a period of difficult adjustment. In parallel, entirely new industries have emerged — computers, software, biotechnology — that depend on skills that didn't exist a decade ago.

During the 1960s, 1970s, and 1980s, the Canadian economy had to create millions of new jobs to provide incomes for the Baby Boomers and for an entire generation of women, whose participation in employment roughly doubled during this period. The wonder is not that unemployment was high at times, but that it was not higher.

In adjusting to these changes, Canada has been living off the social capital generated by the National Projects of the post-war era. That social capital is showing signs of depletion. Six years of intensive deficit-cutting have taken their toll. Far more serious damage has been done by politicians who accidentally or intentionally have destroyed community-based institutions that had been built by previous generations of citizens.

No one can seriously argue that budget-cutting was unnecessary in the 1990s, given the fiscal situation of the federal government and the provinces. The issue is how the cuts were implemented. Over the past two decades, the private sector has learned that through intelligent process redesign, it is possible simultaneously to improve quality, reduce cost, and enhance the resilience of an organization. Unfortunately, some governments got only the cost reduction part right.

The most extreme example is the government of Mike Harris in Ontario. Rather than intelligent process redesign leading to enhanced organizational resilience, the Harris government used a very dull axe and systematically uprooted every major community-based institution. History may eventually show that in this respect, the Harris government has been the most destructive Canada has known.

School boards were forcibly amalgamated, and then stripped of their ability to raise revenue independently of the provincial government. The provincial government is attempting to micro-manage every aspect of education, from the curriculum to how students are evaluated, to the number of teachers in a school, to the hours they spend in the classroom, to the size of schools, and so on. Teachers, who have spent years in training to develop the skills necessary to meet the needs of individual students, have been transformed into pawns of the educational bureaucracy. School trustees, many of whom have provided years of dedicated service to their communities, were treated as leeches on the system. Parents have been promised more influence on "school councils," but about all that is left for these councils to do is raise money to pay for the things the government no longer provides.

Despite the fact that hospitals in Ontario were previously owned by the community and run by community-based boards of directors, the Harris government provoked a health funding crisis and then used its power to unilaterally decide which hospitals should be closed or merged and where new beds should be allocated. Citizens who had provided years of voluntary service on community hospital boards had zero influence on these decisions. This is how much time we can expect prominent and able citizens to dedicate in future when their efforts and abilities are treated with such contempt.

Municipal government financing has been thrust into a state of complete confusion that will take years to sort out. The Harris government forced an amalgamation of the cities that comprised Metro Toronto despite the fact that the citizens of these former cities rejected this idea in a referendum. It then ignored the recommendations of its own task force, and unilaterally reallocated responsibility for funding social services and roads onto municipalities, while taking over full responsibility for education. Municipalities throughout the province are struggling to rebalance their budgets, figure out where the extra tax dollars will come from, and try to appease angry citizens and business people facing double- and, in some cases, triple-digit tax increases.

The Harris government evidently does not recognize the difference between the cost of public services to government and the cost to society, as we discussed in Chapter 3 in relation to health insurance. As a result of their slash-and-burn approach to cutting the cost to government of public services, the overall cost to society of these same public services will start to increase in an uncontrollable fashion.

In parallel with this process of uprooting community-based institu tions, the Harris government has spent millions on misleading, partisan political advertising, all financed by the taxpayers. A recent television commercial depicts a young boy gingerly trying to remove an adhesive bandage from his leg. Rip it off quickly, says his mother, it will hurt less in the long run. This, we are informed by a voice-over, is how the Harris government justifies its heavy-handed unilateral rearrangement of the health care system. This would be funny if it weren't so Orwellian.

The Harris government is an interesting anomaly. While nominally still called the Ontario *Progressive* Conservative Party, the Harris government represents a complete departure from the policies of previous Progressive Conservative governments of the 1950s, 1960s, 1970s, and early 1980s, those led by Leslie Frost, John Robarts, and Bill Davis. Although conservative, these other governments deserved to be called progressive, as they participated actively in the National Projects of the post-war era. Harris, by contrast, is a regressive conservative who is systematically destroying this legacy. No wonder Bill Davis has gone out of his way to distance himself from Harris, as have many other prominent Ontario Tories.

In undermining community-based institutions, the Harris government represents the polar opposite of the kind of government we need in Canada if we are to avoid the futures outlined in Chapter 2. We need governments, of whatever political party, that understand the crucial importance of creating strong community-based organizations. Only strong local orga- nizations are capable of using National Projects to leverage their efforts and resources to create a better future for their citizens.

We invite you to participate in what Albert Einstein used to call a thought experiment. Imagine that between now and 2017, we implemented all the National Projects described in this book. What would be the result?

First, Canada would still be at the top of the United Nations' list of the best places to live. We would have an even healthier population, as a result of having implemented actions to improve the health of all Canadians and having undertaken a major campaign to create the best conditions for the healthy development of all Canada's children.

Far from having a large underclass, we would have an even better-educated population, a result of having the best infrastructure for lifelong learning in the world.

Our economy would be substantially stronger, benefiting as it would from significant shares in the global market for educational new media and a wide range of products incorporating new energy systems. Canadian competitiveness overall would improve through lower health care costs and a healthier population, higher energy efficiency, and a more highly educated and flexible workforce.

We would have recovered quickly from any problems created by the year 2000 computer problem, and would have established a stronger foresight and oversight role with respect to new technologies. We would have continued to strengthen our major societal systems.

The Canadian environment would be substantially improved as a result of lower greenhouse gas emissions. Canada's reputation in the world would be enhanced through its leadership role with new energy systems, population health initiatives, and new media education.

We believe that such a future is possible, despite the forces of globalization and technological change. One National Project by itself cannot create such a future. But a set of National Projects, interacting with each other, can create a powerful force for positive change.

Indeed, this is what happened in the third quarter of the twentieth century. It was the interaction of the Health Care for All project with the Education for All project, the Income Security for All project, the Human Rights for All project, and the Canadian Culture project that created the Canada We Have.

It is the interaction of the Health for All project, with the Healthy Development for All Children project, the New Energy Systems project, the New Media Education project, and the Strengthening Societal Systems project that will make it possible to combat the prevailing global forces to create the Canada We Want.

NATIONAL PROJECTS AND NATIONAL UNITY

Why should we have a country called Canada, occupying more space on the planet than any other except Russia? There was a time when this was a question that most Canadians didn't need to ask or have answered. However, decades of separatism in Quebec and periodic episodes of western alienation make this a question that Canada must now address seriously. While western alienation remains important, the issue of Quebec will, once again, dominate the Canadian political landscape of the early years of the twenty-first century, as Lucien Bouchard and his colleagues attempt to create the "winning conditions" for the next referendum on sovereignty.

Over the past twenty-five years, the Parti Québécois, more recently abetted by its federal allies, the Bloc Québécois, has been busy developing an answer to the question "Why should Quebecers have a country called Quebec?" For the past fifteen years, the federal government's response has swung from proposing changes in the constitution, to talking about what a great country Canada is, to warning of the negative consequences of separation, to ignoring the situation and hoping it would go away on its own. The problem is that all these responses are beside the point.

Constitutional negotiations do not answer the question of why we should have a country. They deal with three entirely different questions: what are the rights of the individual in relation to the state; how we should govern ourselves; and how we should divide up powers among different levels of government. Most constitutional negotiations in the past few decades have been about the power-sharing issue. Even the negotiations around the Charter of Rights and Freedoms, which should have been about the rights of individuals in relation to the state, got caught up in a fight about the rights of provinces to pass legislation "notwithstanding" the provisions of the charter. Federal-provincial negotiations over the past few decades have rarely focused on what the objects of the exercise of government power should be, or on how the federal government and the provinces could collaborate to achieve common objectives.

To Quebecers intrigued by the idea of a country called Quebec, "I Love Canada" speeches are irrelevant. Separatists are not interested in what a great country Canada is. They take for granted what they now have, and focus instead on painting a grand picture of what it will be like when they have all this and sovereignty too — whatever that means.

Threatening Quebecers with the consequences of separation, no matter how accurate the forecast, will not work. The arguments have become stale and blunted by repetition. Ignoring the problem is tempting, but obviously self-defeating.

There is still one strategy that we haven't yet tried, but it may be the only one left. Let's call it Plan Z. This strategy involves laying out a detailed, positive vision for Canada's future, and organizing a set of National Projects — probably about five to eight in total — that offers a credible way to achieve that vision.

This set of National Projects should describe a series of specific goals that, if accomplished, would add significantly to the quality of life of all Canadians, and of children and grandchildren yet to come. It should be evident to Canadians that no single province or region, acting alone, could achieve these goals.

While this approach will be attractive to many Canadians, it will be especially appealing to the younger generation. Canadian youth are eager to have a positive outlet for their desire to do something good for their society. A recent poll in Quebec showed that young people are fed up with constitutional negotiations — what they want to talk about are *projets de société*.

Of course, national unity is not the only, or even the primary, reason we should implement a set of National Projects. We should decide on each National Project on its own merits, based on its likely contribution to the well-being of citizens, to the economy, and to sustainable development. However, a strong set of National Projects would be a credible answer to the question "Why should we have a country called Canada in the first decades of the twenty-first century?"

Having a new answer to this question would create an enormous challenge for Lucien Bouchard and others who wish to persuade their compatriots to leave Canada. He would be forced to articulate an equal or better vision with equal or better credibility, which would be impossible. The resources of Quebec cannot match the combined resources of Canada. He would be forced to confront the possibility that maybe Canada is a real country after all. More important, however, it can be credibly argued by federalists that the adoption of a new set of National Projects represents a profound recognition by all of Canada of the unique contribution of current generations of Quebecers to the federation.

While National Projects were fading away in the mid-1970s in the rest of Canada, they were gaining ground in Quebec. As noted in Chapter 3, Quebec evolved its own set of "national" projects and used them effectively to develop its economy and society in the 1970s, 1980s, and into the 1990s. It could not fail to create a positive impression among many Quebecers if Canada were to position its new set of National Projects as adopting some of Quebec's own recent strategies, but applying them to Canada as a whole.

If, despite our best efforts, Quebecers vote to separate, we still need to know why we should have a country called Canada in the first decades of the twenty-first century. In fact, in the political and economic crisis that would follow separation, it would be even more urgent to have an answer to this question.

NATIONAL PROJECTS AND THE SOCIAL UNION

"I look at the social union movement and I say, 'It's brilliant. Quebec can't lose,'" former Quebec premier Jacques Parizeau was reported as saying two days before the November 30, 1998, Quebec election. His reasoning:

> Case one: Assuming the federal government agrees to that proposition. Then we can simply say: "We're opting out. Bring on the full financial compensation."
>
> Case two: The provinces abandon us, in the sense that the federal government refuses and the provinces cave in. Quebec turns around to the provinces and says: "You see, we can't trust you." And that perhaps marks the appearance of the first winning conditions. . . . We could say, you see, there is no way we could agree. We have to get out of this country. So we can't lose. It is the type of amazing situation where in any case, it plays into Quebec's hands.

Canada has its provincial premiers — all of them — to thank for creating this amazing lose-lose situation for Canada. The social union talks were originally to be about how the federal government and the provinces could strengthen social policy in Canada. Initially, the topics under discussion included the National Child Benefit, the National Children's Agenda described in Chapter 7, and increasing benefits and services for Canadians with disabilities.

In the spring and summer of 1998, however, the premiers hijacked the process with three principal demands. The first was that no new social policy initiatives should be considered until Ottawa had reversed the cuts that were made to provincial transfers in its quest for a balanced budget in the late 1990s. The second was that any new national social program should require the consent of the majority of the provinces. The third was that any province or territory should have the right to opt out of any new or modified Canada-wide social program in areas of provincial jurisdiction, while still receiving full funding from the federal government, provided a program with similar objectives was introduced. The premiers have so far rejected the idea that provinces that opt out should be required to perform to national standards, and that there should be consequences for failing to perform to those standards.

When Bouchard saw this coming, he reversed decades of Quebec boycotting of federal-provincial negotiations and hurried out to Saskatoon in August 1998 to join the other premiers and make their demands unanimous. He could recognize a turkey served up on a silver platter as well as anyone. In his acceptance speech after the November 30, 1998, Quebec election, he promised to press ahead with the social union agenda as quickly as possible. He knew that Parizeau was absolutely correct. No matter whether the premiers' collective demands are accepted or rejected by the federal government, it is one more step towards winning conditions for the next referendum.

What is wrong with this picture? The problem is that the provinces and the federal government are arguing about process without content. The discussions are about jurisdictions defined by the 1867 British North America Act, who gets to collect taxes, and how much of the taxes collected by the federal government should be transferred to the provinces. What's missing is any serious consideration of the national interest. By the term "national interest," we are not referring to the interests of the federal government. We mean the interests of the Canadian nation, of us thirty million Canadians. Who is speaking for us in the social union talks?

Let us acknowledge and respect the fact that the premiers were in part acting out of legitimate frustrations with the status quo. In part, their position was a reaction to the introduction in the 1998 budget of the

Millennium Scholarship Fund, a good idea that was implemented badly, with no previous consultation to make sure that it complemented the various provincial approaches to support for university and college students. Some premiers were making a point about western alienation. Some premiers saw this as a way to impose greater fiscal conservatism on Canada as a whole, by making it harder to introduce new social programs. All saw it as a way to strengthen their position in the endless Canadian power-struggle we call intergovernmental relations.

Let us also acknowledge that there has to be room for innovation and flexibility in the Canadian federation. But that, fundamentally, is the problem with the position taken by the premiers. If the arrangements the premiers recommend had been in place in the 1950s, Canadians would not have got universal health insurance, or at least not so quickly. We would have not seen the same progress on income security. The premiers seem to have forgotten that many of the most important characteristics of Canadian society today rest on the foundation laid by previous generations who agreed with the Rowell-Sirois Commission that it is the essence of Canada to ensure that Canadians, no matter where they live, enjoy comparable public services.

From our own history, we can conclude that one of the virtues of a federal system is to spread innovation, wherever it comes from, across the country. To make it almost as hard to introduce new social programs as it is to amend the constitution is nuts.

The most important reason that the federal government cannot agree to the premiers' demands in their current form is that they would make it impossible for Canada to implement any of the National Projects described in this book. The premiers' position implies that we have to restore full funding to health care before we can start to talk about doing something about developmental health or undertaking a major initiative on Canada's children. Because new energy systems and educational new media touch on areas of provincial jurisdiction, we could end up with a patchwork quilt of disconnected, provincial approaches, instead of a strong, collective national approach — hardly a good foundation for succeeding in global markets. Effectively, we would be locked into existing programs and structures.

Before we go much further with the social union process, we need first to talk about what we want to achieve as a nation over the coming few decades. It will be easier to be flexible about fiscal arrangements if we are first in agreement about what we're trying to accomplish collectively. Prime Minister Jean Chrétien is absolutely correct when he says that Canadians don't want to talk about the constitution, but we believe they are ready for a conversation about National Projects. Remember the Ekos poll, referred to in Chapter 7, which found that more than 86 percent thought it was important for the government to produce a list of National Projects that could serve as goals for Canadian society.

So how would Canadians respond if we asked the right questions? If we share with Canadians what we know about developmental health, and ask whether as a society we should take collective action to improve the developmental health of all Canadians, what would the answer be?

Given what we know about the developmental health of children in particular, if we ask whether as a society we should take action to ensure that all children are ready to learn by the age of six, what would the answer be?

Given what we know about greenhouse gases and climate change, and given that we have Canadian technologies that address these very problems, if we ask Canadians whether we should make a major effort to transform energy systems in Canada, and ultimately throughout the world, to ones that are more efficient and more compatible with sustainable development, what would the answer be?

Given that we are, in John Ralston Saul's words, "a coalition of ideas based on an assumption of the public good," if we ask Canadians whether we should make a major effort to implement lifelong learning, put our knowledge and culture on the Internet, and share what we know and who we are with the rest of the world, what would the answer be?

We believe that, if asked, Canadians would answer the above, and similar questions about other National Projects, in the affirmative. We hope someone will ask these questions, soon.

We also believe Canadians instinctively understand that they benefit from a federal system that does not result in a lowest-common-denominator approach to governance, and that the collaboration, and even at times the competition and conflict, among governments creates positive synergy that results in better outcomes than if we had only one level of government.

This is obvious to Quebecers above all. They know that they benefit from being part of a nation called Canada, even while they are also part of a distinct society — aw, what the hell, let's agree to call it a nation — called Quebec. Does there have to be a conflict between the two? If nationality is defined by a perception of the mutual obligations that exist among members of a society, and how those obligations are articulated through the political process and are communicated through arts, literature, and popular culture, do Quebecers have to make a choice between being members of the Canadian nation and members of the Quebec nation? Can they not be, in Jean Charest's words, proud Quebecers and proud Canadians? Quebecers are tired of being forced by the separatists to choose one or the other. The rest of Canada should not force this choice either.

Jean Charest's most important message to Quebecers in the last Quebec election campaign was that we have to stop the nonsense. We have to stop arguing about money and powers and focus first on outcomes. Whether our strategies are working in the best interests of people, not governments or political parties. Whether we are achieving the best results we can as a society. If the evidence proves that we're not, then we need the courage to abandon worn-out ideas and change course. Charest's message to Quebecers deserves to be listened to carefully by all of Canada.

Why don't we simply agree that we want Canada to continue to be recognized as the best society in the world, and just get on with it?

Toronto and Colborne
December 1, 1998

An Invitation

We encourage Canadians to visit the Canada We Want website (http://canada.matrixlinks.ca) and join the conspiracy.

Let us know what you think of the ideas in this book, and contribute your own thoughts about National Projects and Strategic Opportunities. The website also includes additional background information, links to the websites of organizations mentioned in the book, updates on some of the issues discussed, and where possible, links to original source documents.

John Godfrey can be reached by email at jgodfrey@matrixlinks.ca. Rob McLean can be reached at rmclean@matrixlinks.ca.

Resources

The following list of selected documents and websites includes URLs that were current at the time this list was compiled. As a convenience to our readers, the Canada We Want website at http://canada.matrixlinks.ca includes a chapter-by-chapter listing of links to organizations mentioned and source documents available on the Internet.

Books, Articles, and Reports

Angell, Ian. "The Information Revolution and the Death of the State." London, 1995. http://www.illusions.com/TheUniverse/Info-Revolution.htm

_____. "The Real Politik of the Information Age." London, January 1998. http://techpolicy.lse.ac.uk/csrc/crypto/real-politik/htm

_____. "The Signs Are Clear: The Future Is Inequality." London, October 1996. http://visionarymarketing.com/signs.html

Barlow, Maude, and James Winter. *The Big Black Book: The Essential Views of Conrad Black and Barbara Amiel.* Toronto: Stoddart, 1997.

Biggs, Margaret. "Building Blocks for Canada's New Social Union." *Canadian Policy Research Networks Working Paper*, no. F/02/ (1996).

Black, Conrad. *A Life in Progress.* Toronto: Key Porter Books, 1993.

_____. "Canadian Capers." *The National Interest*, no. 28 (summer 1992).

_____. "Taking Canada Seriously." *International Journal* 53, no. 1 (winter 1997/98): 1–16.

Bothwell, Robert. *A Short History of Ontario*. Edmonton: Hurtig, 1986.

Campaign 2000. "Mission for the Millennium: A Comprehensive Strategy for Children and Youth." *Discussion Paper*, no. 2 (November 1997).

Canadian Council on Social Development. *Talking with Canadians: Citizen Engagement and the Social Union*. July 1998.

Careless, J. M. S. *Canada: A Story of Challenge*. Toronto: Macmillan, 1970.

Drucker, Peter. "The Age of Social Transformation." *The Atlantic Monthly* (November 1994): 53–80.

Evans, Robert G., Morris L. Barer, and Theodore R. Marmor, eds. *Why Are Some People Healthy and Others Not? The Determinants of Health of Populations*. New York: A. de Gruyter, 1994.

Fallows, James. *Looking at the Sun: The Rise of the New East Asian Economic and Political System*. New York: Pantheon, 1994.

Fraser, Matthew. *Quebec Inc.: French-Canadian Entrepreneurs and the New Business Elite*. Toronto: Key Porter Books, 1987.

Gibson, William. "Johnny Mnemonic." In *Burning Chrome*. Toronto: HarperCollins, 1995.

_____. *Count Zero*. New York: Ace Books, 1986.

_____. *Mona Lisa Overdrive*. New York: Bantam Books, 1988.

_____. *Neuromancer*. Toronto: HarperCollins, 1995.

Godfrey, John. "Community or Solitude?" Paper read at Couchiching Summer Conference, Orillia, Ontario, 1996.

_____. "A Proposed Post-Referendum Strategy for the Federal Government." 10 November 1995. Available on John Godfrey's website at http://www.johngodfrey.on.ca

_____, ed. "National Projects for a New Canada." Conference Summary, 2 March 1996. Available on John Godfrey's website at http://www.johngodfrey.on.ca

Hoffmann, Peter, ed. *Hydrogen and Fuel Cell Letter*.

http://www.mhv.net/~hfcletter

Hunter, David. *It's Your Turn*. Committee on Youth to the Secretary of State, 1971.

Keating, Daniel P., and Clyde Hertzman, eds. *Developmental Health and the Wealth of Nations: Social, Biological, and Educational Dynamics*. New York: Guilford Press, 1999.

Lapham, Lewis. "Notebook: Swiss Pastry." *Harper's* (June 1998): 10–15.

Martin, Paul. "Rethinking Canada for the 21st Century." Paper read at Couchiching Summer Conference, Orillia, Ontario, 1998.

McLean, Robert I. G. *Performance Measures in the New Economy*. Toronto: The Premier's Council, 1995.

McNaught, Kenneth. *The Penguin History of Canada*. Toronto: Penguin, 1988.

McQuaig, Linda. *The Cult of Impotence: Selling the Myth of Powerlessness in the Global Economy*. Toronto: Viking, 1998.

Olive, David. "Listening to Quebec." *Report on Business Magazine* (February 1996).

Ontario Hospital Services Commission. *Annual Reports*. 1960 and 1961.

Ontario Premier's Council. *Ontario 2002*. Toronto, 1993.

Organization for Economic Co-operation and Development. *Economic Survey of Canada*. Paris, November 1997.

Report of the Royal Commission on the Economic Union and Development Prospects for Canada. Ottawa: Ministry of Supply and Services, 1985.

Report of the Royal Commission on National Development in the Arts, Letters, and Sciences, 1951. Available on the National Library of Canada website at http://www.nlc-bnc.ca/massey/rpt/etable.htm, courtesy of SchoolNet Digital Collections at http://www.schoolnet.ca/collections/E/index.htm

Saul, John Ralston. *Reflections of a Siamese Twin: Canada at the End of the Twentieth Century*. Toronto: Viking, 1996.

Siklos, Richard. *Shades of Black: Conrad Black and the World's Fastest Growing Press Empire*. Toronto: Minerva Canada, 1995.

Standing Committee on Human Resources Development and the Status of Persons with Disabilities. "National Roundtable on Children, Prenatal to Six Years: Readiness to Learn." 11 June 1998.

Tarnopolsky, Walter S. *The Canadian Bill of Rights*. Toronto: McClelland and Stewart, 1975.

Torjman, Sherri. *Civil Society: Reclaiming Our Humanity*. Ottawa: Caledon Institute, 1997.

TWU Transmitter. "Without Strong Government Intervention We Face a Bleak Future" (editorial).

United Nations Human Development Program. *Human Development Report 1998*. Available at http://www.undp.org/hdro

Urquhart, R. W. Ian. "The Doctor and the Plan." *Ontario Medical Review* 25, no. 7 (July 1958).

Vipond, Robert C. *Liberty and Community: Canadian Federalism and the Failure of the Constitution*. Albany: State University of New York Press, 1991.

Woodcock, George. *A Social History of Canada*. Toronto: Viking, 1988.

Websites

Ballard Power Systems
    http://www.ballard.com
British Columbia Ministry of Environment, Lands, and Parks
    http://www.env.gov.bc.ca
Canadian Heritage
    http://www.pch.gc.ca
Canadian Institute of Chartered Accountants and the Canadian
Performance Reporting Initiative
    http://www.cica.ca
Energy Council of Canada
    http://www.energy.ca
Environment Canada
    http://www.ec.gc.ca

Health Canada

   http://www.hc-sc.gc.ca

National Children's Agenda Caucus Committee

   http://www.johngodfrey.on.ca/childagenda.htm

National Climate Change Process

   http://www.nccp.ca

National Energy Board

   http://www.neb.gc.ca

New Flyer

   http://www.newflyer.com

Office of Technology Assessment reports archive

   http://www.ota.nap.edu

SchoolNet

   http://www.schoolnet.ca

Shell UK

   http://www.shell.co.uk

Acknowledgements

The ideas in this book evolved over many years, and were stimulated by many discussions, conversations, and the work of others. Any errors or omissions are, of course, the responsibility of the authors.

In addition to our children, this book is dedicated to Fraser Mustard, whose vision and network-building is a source of hope and inspiration to a vast collection of "FOF's," among whom we are proud to be included.

Andrew Bevan, John Godfrey's executive assistant, pushed John to write the book, then worked closely with John and Rob during the research and writing phases.

John Godfrey thanks his wife, Trish Bongard, an early advocate of the project, for her constant love, support, and understanding, particularly during the writing phase of the book, which diminished family time on holidays, weekends, and evenings.

Valuable comments on the draft text were provided by Don Bastian and his colleagues at Stoddart, Stephen Clarkson, John Coleman, John

English, Paul Genest, Sophia Huyer, Dan Keating, Stephen Marcus, Paul Martin, Fraser Mustard, Gerald Owen, and Rob Vipond.

In addition, Rob McLean wishes to acknowledge the following individuals who contributed, directly or indirectly, to the ideas in the book: Tom Brzustowski, Paul Cantor, Bruce Fountain, Michael Gibbons, Jonathan Guss, Brent Herbert-Copley, Chaviva Hosek, David Hunter, Frankie Liberty, Ron McCullough, Peg McLean, Peter Milner, John Mitsopoulos, John de la Mothe, Peter Nicholson, Geoff Oldham, Rob Paterson, Bob Rae, Debby Roman, Terry Sullivan, Peter Timmerman, Don Urquhart, Henry Voss, Fraser Wilson, and David Wolfe.

Index

About the Authors

John Godfrey

John Godfrey is the Liberal member of Parliament for the federal riding of Don Valley West in Toronto. He currently chairs the National Children's Agenda Caucus, as well as the Children and Youth at Risk Sub-Committee of the Standing Committee on Human Resources Development and the Status of Persons with Disabilities. He has been chairman of two other Standing Committees, Canadian Heritage and Industry, as well as Parliamentary Secretary to the Ministers of International Cooperation and Canadian Heritage. He was educated at the University of Toronto and earned his M.Phil. and D.Phil. in Modern European History from Oxford University. In 1987, he published *Capitalism at War*, a major study of French economic mobilization in the First World War. He was previously president of the University of King's College in Halifax, editor of the *Financial Post*, and vice-president of the Canadian Institute for Advanced Research. He lives in Toronto with his wife, Trish Bongard, and their son, Ian.

Rob McLean

As president of MatrixLinks International Inc., Rob McLean advises corporations, research institutions, and governments on strategic responses to systemic change. Born in Manitoba, he received an M.A. in political theory at the University of Toronto, and became a Chartered Accountant and Certified Management Consultant while working at Clarkson Gordon and Woods Gordon. He has experience in the private, public, and research sectors as a strategy consulting partner with Ernst & Young, executive director of the Ontario Premier's Council, and executive director of the International Federation of Institutes for Advanced Study. His work has taken him to more than thirty-five developed and developing countries, and all parts of Canada. He has written numerous studies and reports, and speaks regularly to business and public sector audiences about strategy, policy, and performance. McLean lives on a sheep farm east of Toronto, and is an enthusiastic sailor, musician, and father of three teenagers. In previous elections, he has voted Liberal, Tory, New Democrat, and Rhinoceros.